Longing
for My Child

Longing
for My Child

Reflections for Parents and Siblings
after a Child's Death

Christine O'Keeffe Lafser

LOYOLAPRESS.

3441 N. ASHLAND AVENUE
CHICAGO, ILLINOIS 60657

Unless otherwise indicated, Scripture quotations contained herein are from the New Revised Standard Version Bible: Catholic Edition, copyright © 1993 and 1989 by the Division of Christian Education of the National Council of Churches of Christ in the U.S.A. Used by permission. All rights reserved.

Scripture excerpts marked (NAB) are taken from the *New American Bible with Revised New Testament and Psalms,* copyright © 1991, 1986, 1970 by the Confraternity of Christian Doctrine, Inc., Washington, D.C. Used with permission. All rights reserved. No part of the *New American Bible* may be reproduced by any means without permission in writing from the copyright owner.

"Our Long Dark Forest" is reprinted from *What to Do When the Police Leave: A Guide to the First Days of Traumatic Loss* by Bill Jenkins (Richmond, Va.: W.B.J. Press, 2001). Used with permission of Bill Jenkins.

Interior template by Lisa Buckley

Library of Congress Cataloging-in-Publication Data
Lafser, Christine O'Keeffe.
    Longing for my child: reflections for parents and siblings after a
    child's death / Christine O'Keeffe Lafser.
      p. cm.
    Includes bibliographical references.
    ISBN 0-8294-1754-0
    1. Bereavement—Religious aspects—Christianity—Meditations. 2.
Parents—Religious life. I. Title.

    BV4905.3 .L34 2000
    242'.4—dc21

                                2001050792

Printed in the United States
02 03 04 05 06 Bang 10 9 8 7 6 5 4 3 2 1

This book is dedicated
to my husband, Bill,
who shows his love and support
in countless ways every day.

In his caring eyes,
his hardworking hands,
and his tender arms,
I know the love of God.

I am utterly spent and crushed;
   I groan because of the tumult of my heart.

O Lord, all my longing is known to you;
   my sighing is not hidden from you.

PSALM 38:8–9

CONTENTS

One of the things I have unwillingly learned this past month is that grief changes things. We will grow through it; we will mature through it; we will learn more about ourselves and those around us than we ever wanted to know; we will reorder our priorities. What once was of vital importance to us is as dull as mud, and what we never appreciated to its fullest we find to be more valuable than gold. Yet through it all, we will survive. We will get stronger, and we will find the answers for ourselves that seem to work best for us.

We are all shuffling through a dark forest together, one tiny step at a time. We hold the hands of those walking with us; we try to follow the faint footsteps of those who passed this way before us. Sometimes we stumble and fall, and we are glad that there is someone there to help us up. They help us get cleaned up and back on our feet, yet at the same time the process of getting back up simply serves to put us back on our inexorable journey again.

Once in a while we see a patch of light through the canopy, and we bask in it as if we had never seen light before, for we do not know how long it will last, nor when we shall come across the next patch of brightness on the forest floor. We do not know for how many miles this forest extends. Yet through it all, we survive. It is a long journey; it is a fearful journey, but I am assured that it is not so dark at our destination as it seems now.

Bill Jenkins
What to Do When the Police Leave: A Guide to the First Days of Traumatic Loss

*T*here are few things in
life as devastating to a family as the death of a child.
When my children died, I didn't believe I could ever be
happy again. Now, years later, although I am forever
changed and I still miss them every day, I am finally
capable of happiness. I still have good days and bad
days, but the good days are more frequent, and the bad
days are now rare. I offer these pages in the hope that
they will be helpful to other parents and siblings who
have suffered a painful loss. I hope that these words
provide reassurance as you grieve, as well as a glimmer
of hope for your future.

Whether your child's death was violent or peaceful;
sudden or prolonged; a result of disease; an accident, a
murder, or a suicide; or of undetermined cause;
whether your child was young or old or somewhere in
between, I hope you will find comfort, support, and

encouragement in these short reflections. Many are based on my experiences and those of my family after the deaths of my children. Others reflect the experiences of other grieving parents and siblings. Some of the circumstances of these children's lives and deaths are detailed in the Profiles section; others are mentioned or alluded to in the reflections themselves. My special thanks go to many of the parents and families who are part of the Richmond chapter of Compassionate Friends. These families generously shared their own stories and experiences, reliving the pain of their children's deaths in an effort to make this book helpful to other grieving parents.

The grief process does not proceed in a straight line from despair to hope. Some days will be almost unbearable; others will be much better. Healing takes time, probably more time than you think and definitely more time than the people around you ever dreamed. I can't encourage you enough to allow yourself to grieve in your own way, at your own pace, and to use this book in whatever way helps you most: taking in a few random pages at a time, reading straight through from beginning to end, or stopping at pages that express just how you feel or that will help you find hope for tomorrow. Above all, I urge you to pay particular attention to the Scripture verses, for it is in them that I think you will find real consolation.

You can help your spouse, your parents, your children, and others better understand what you are going through by sharing passages of this book that particularly express how you feel. Often men, women, and children grieve very differently, and this can be a source of conflict and resentment if it is not understood. Being able to share our grief with one another and talk about the feelings and experiences that accompanied that grief united our family in a whole new way after our children died. Although our expressions of grief and ways of dealing with it were very different, they were appropriate and, eventually, healing for each of us.

It may also help to share these passages with people who want to help you. It is my hope that doctors, nurses, priests, ministers, counselors, relatives, and friends may also find in these pages the insight needed to better understand, minister to, and help those who grieve. I have learned from experience that many people need to learn insight and empathy when it comes to relating to people who grieve. I have heard many ludicrous comments and witnessed others' strange ways of dealing with—or not dealing with—grieving friends and family members.

It is widely believed that the death of a child is likely to destroy the marriage of the parents.

Even though research has shown that this is not true, this "fact" continues to be quoted over and over. Many marriages and families actually become stronger after such a tragedy. As you and your spouse suffer together in your grief for your child, you may find that you not only are binding up each other's wounds but also are more deeply interweaving your lives and the lives of your family members than you ever could have without such tribulation. Sharing the pain and surviving it together can ultimately bring you closer to each other, although you may have to endure some rough times first. Perhaps this is part of the redemptive nature of suffering.

Healing does eventually come. You will not always feel the way you do now. Although you will be forever changed, you will one day be able to see the beauty and enjoy the goodness of this world again.

It is my desire that this book will help bring
you to God in a new way, strengthening and
renewing your faith, even in the face of such
deep sorrow. I hope it will console you to
remember that God loves each of us as we love
our own children and that he wants to hold us
in his loving arms as we grieve. We need only
turn to his embrace.

~ PROFILES

Ann

Young Child Who Died of Cancer

Ann loved to swing on the swings and play in the sandbox in the backyard. Being outdoors was her greatest joy. I can still see her snaggletoothed grin as she squints up at me in the sunshine, pedaling for all she is worth on her pink tricycle.

~ 2   I was surprised one beautiful spring day when she told me that she was too tired to go outside and instead went to lie down on her bed. When I checked on her a few minutes later, she was sound asleep. At first I thought she must have had a very busy morning in kindergarten, but a few days and several naps later, I began to be concerned. When she declined her daddy's horsey ride after supper because she was "just too tired," I decided to call the pediatrician's office as soon as it opened the next morning.

After weeks of tests and waiting for one result after another, they found the tumor. Surgery was next, followed by radiation and then chemotherapy. We hoped and prayed for a miracle. There were X-rays and CAT scans and MRIs. There were blood tests and endless IVs and more procedures than could be imagined. Many of them were painful. Most of them were scary. We rejoiced when we heard "remission," only to despair again a few short months later when we heard "reoccurrence." We endured more radiation, more chemotherapy, more procedures, and always the endless waiting, the comparison to other results, the search for small signs of improvement and hope. Although there were many miracles throughout the process, the cure we hoped for didn't materialize. Our little Ann died the following spring, on another bright sunny day, when she should have been playing in the backyard.

Chris

Young Adult Killed in a Sporting Accident

Almost every weekend, Chris went kayaking with his buddies. He had taken up the sport when he was a junior in college and had been kayaking regularly for about five years. He was very safety conscious and responsible—he always wore his helmet and life jacket and followed all the safety precautions. Although his father and I worried about him, we were glad that he sought his thrills in wholesome outdoor activities rather than in other, less healthy avenues. Chris was an Eagle Scout, so I knew that he had at least some knowledge of how to take care of himself in the great outdoors.

He was so excited about his upcoming trip. It was going to be a ten-day white-water adventure that included sections of the Chattooga River. Chris and his friends had been planning it and looking forward to it for months. Chris had decided that he would drive home a day earlier than his friends so that he could attend the college graduation of his brother, Eric, at the College of William and Mary, Chris's own alma mater. Instead, the graduation turned out to be the day after Chris's funeral.

One beautiful day on the river, as Chris and his friends were scouting a rapid, one of his friend's paddles slipped away from him, and Chris set out to retrieve it. Shortly afterward, Chris's kayak got caught in the hydraulic of the rapid, and he had to make a wet exit. While trying to free the kayak, he was pulled underwater by the hydraulic. His friends saw him bob up briefly, drift into quieter water, and then disappear as he was swept through another rapid. After hours of searching, they found his bruised and rigid body several miles downstream.

We got the phone call sometime between 9:00 and 10:00 P.M. I had just fallen asleep when the phone rang. We had gone to bed early after working on some special projects around the house.

Our younger son, Eric, had gone to the beach for a few days between exams and graduation. We didn't have the phone number for the place where he was staying but were finally able to track him down before the night was over. In those few hours between 9:00 P.M. and midnight, all our lives changed forever.

Luke

Neonatal Death

I found out I was pregnant a few days before
Christmas. We were so excited and happy. Caleb
was going to be a big brother, and we were going
to have another precious baby. The ultrasound at
seventeen weeks revealed that the baby was a boy.
We decided to name him Luke. It was nice to have
a name for him so early and to talk to him and
think of him as our Luke.

I had some rather severe abdominal pain one
Saturday night in February, but the doctor reassured
me that everything was fine. The Sunday after the
St. Patrick's Day parade, we went to dinner at my
in-laws' house. While we were eating, I started
feeling very bad and again had severe abdominal
pains. My husband postponed his business trip
that was scheduled for the next day, and I went to
the doctor. There was some concern that I might

have appendicitis, but nothing definite was revealed upon examination. The doctor again assured me that everything seemed to be OK, in spite of the pain I was experiencing. He advised me to take it easy, so I closed the full-time day-care service that I had been providing in my home.

I continued to have pain off and on. Instead of diminishing, it just got worse. By April the pain was so severe that it hurt to walk. I had a difficult time getting off the couch and was sleeping very little because I couldn't get comfortable in any position. The nausea was so great that I wasn't able to eat the food that I knew my baby needed. The doctor didn't seem to understand the severity of the pain and tried to explain it away as ligament pain that sometimes results as the expanding uterus puts pressure on the abdominal ligaments.

One night in early May the pain was so bad, and we were so frustrated, that my husband called the

doctor's office and told them I was in labor. We met
the doctor at the hospital, where it was determined
that I was having contractions but none were big
enough to explain the amount of pain I was having.
For three days they did all kinds of tests and called
in specialists, but nobody could find a cause for my
pain. There were renal tests and gastric procedures
and ultrasounds. My appendix and kidneys were
normal, and Luke looked good. With no definitive
diagnosis the obstetrician said I could go home after
supper. Since it was so late, and I was still no better,
my mother, who is a nurse whom the doctor knew,
suggested that he keep me in the hospital overnight
to see how my body handled the food. Our son,
Caleb, was with his grandparents, and my husband
was so concerned about Luke and me that he
decided to stay with me at the hospital. By
10:00 P.M. the pain was excruciating. I tried walking
the halls; I couldn't be still. No position lessened
the pain. At 2:00 A.M. I went to the bathroom, and
I was bleeding. I called the nurse, who checked me

and told the other nurse to call the doctor. She reported that he wasn't coming in. My nurse told her that the doctor had better come in, because I was eight centimeters dilated and was going to have this baby. We learned that the placenta was separating from the uterus. I was glad that I was at the hospital, where I could be taken care of properly; otherwise I could have bled to death.

Our precious little Luke was born just a couple of hours later. Our pastor was there to baptize him. They put him in a warmer and took him to the nursery. Later they brought him back in a portable incubator, and I was able to look at him. He was tiny but perfect. He had white hair, and his legs and feet were just like his big brother's. He had his daddy's hands. At twenty-four weeks his little eyes were fused shut, so I don't know if they were brown like mine or blue like his father's. They said that he looked big for twenty-four weeks. He might have a chance. I wanted to hold him, but I was afraid to touch him. I didn't want to give him any germs. They transported him to another hospital in town that had a neonatal intensive care unit. I couldn't go with him, but my husband followed the transport to the hospital and stayed with Luke. His lungs were insufficiently developed, and he was having a hard time. He was already having seizures, and his heart had begun to fail when he reached the NICU. His little body just wasn't developed enough to survive in this big world. Luke lived for only about eight hours after he was born. He died in his daddy's arms. I helped him into the world, and his daddy was there to help him out of it. His life experience was so short—so much shorter than we would have wanted.

When we came home from the hospital, we realized that it had rained. The flowers were blooming, and everything was bright and beautiful. That radiant spring green that you see at no other time was all around us. It occurred to me that anyone looking at us riding in our car would have no idea of the heartache we were feeling or that we had just experienced the death of our precious baby. I try hard not to judge when somebody cuts me off in traffic, or is rude, because I realize that you never know what might be happening in someone else's life.

Our dreams are simpler now, but our faith is stronger. Luke was our baby for only a short time, but we celebrate the time that we had with him. Every day we are glad that he was our son and grateful that we have an angel baby watching over us, a child born of our love for each other.

After a spring rain, when the flowers are freshly washed and the foliage is bright and green, I'm glad that Luke will never feel the way I am feeling. He will never know pain and grief.

God gave us a wonderful gift when he gave us our little Luke. Although we miss him and wish he could be here with us, growing strong and tall, we believe our family is closer because of the tragedy we have shared. At least, that's how we choose to look at it.

Bobby
Miscarried Baby

It was December 17. I was a little anxious about
the doctor's appointment. At the last appointment
the doctor hadn't heard the baby's heartbeat on
the Doppler. He had assured me that there was
nothing to be concerned about, that it was still
early and not unusual to be unable to detect a
heartbeat at that point. I asked my husband, Bill,
to come with me to this appointment, and I was
glad to have him by my side.

Once again there was no heartbeat. The doctor
immediately arranged for an ultrasound at the
outpatient department. After I drank what seemed
to be gallons of water and we nervously waited and
prayed for what seemed to be hours, we were
ushered into the ultrasound room. I was so scared
for my baby. The ultrasound technician turned
the monitor away from us so that we couldn't see

the image of our baby. She was absorbed in her
work, terse and distant, speaking only to give curt
instructions. When I asked a question, she made it
clear that I should not interrupt her work. When
the radiologist came in a few minutes later, she
introduced herself, spoke briefly to the technician,
peered at the screen, straightened up, and said, "I
can detect no heartbeat. You can go get dressed
now. I will contact your doctor, and you can discuss
it with him." Why didn't they talk to me? Why
didn't they let me see my baby on the screen? Why
were they in such a hurry to get me out of there?

I remember struggling to put on my clothes in the
tiny cubicle in the hall and finally having to ask my
husband for help. Somehow we made it back
upstairs to the doctor's office, where we waited
for him to be available to speak to us. The doctor
finally met with us in a cramped little room. I was
trying hard not to cry but was unsuccessful. He
rattled off some statistics about the prevalence of

15 ~

miscarriage and asked if we would like to schedule the D & C for sometime during the next few days or wait and let nature take its course. Bill asked if there was any danger in waiting. I was still hoping against hope that our baby was alive, despite the evidence to the contrary. Of course, we chose to wait. The doctor told us what to expect.

The next ten days were the worst of my life. It is difficult to function knowing that you are carrying a dead baby, waiting for the inevitable miscarriage to occur and at the same time hoping for the miracle that will bring your baby to life. Everywhere I went and everything I did, I knew that the severe cramping and bleeding could start at any time. I remember running into a neighbor while standing in line with our one-year-old son waiting to see Santa Claus. She knew that I was pregnant and asked about the baby and how I was feeling. It was the first time I had to tell someone outside my family that our baby was dead and that I was waiting to miscarry. I tried to act as normal as possible for our son's sake. He was too little to understand my sadness and my tears.

Christmas was a nightmare, from beginning to end. My parents and my sister came over early in the morning to have breakfast and watch our son open his presents. I remember wanting to scream, "My baby is dead! My baby is dead! Don't you understand?" I was in no frame of mind to celebrate Christmas or be the hostess. I longed for a quiet day with just the three of us; but it seemed selfish, when they wanted so much to see Ben open his presents. My brother had invited the entire family to his house for Christmas dinner. We declined, but the rest of the family called to persuade us to go. "It will be good for you." "You have to eat anyway." "I'm sure you don't feel like fixing anything." "It's Christmas, your husband and son should have a nice meal." I finally capitulated, and we went to the dinner, where we pretended to be OK in order to avoid spoiling everyone else's Christmas.

The strong cramping and heavy bleeding began at eleven o'clock and became progressively severe as the night wore on. At one point I called the hospital and discovered that the doctor I liked the least was on call that night. I was determined to avoid the hospital emergency room until he was off duty. I didn't want to lose my baby with a doctor I couldn't stand. I spent the night moving the ten or twelve feet from the bed to the bathroom, alternately pouring blood into the toilet and searching for tiny baby parts to put in a clean jar, and lying down for a few minutes or seconds until the next horrifying wave of pain hit, bringing with it a new deluge of blood. When I briefly passed out next to the bed around sunrise, Bill said that he didn't care who was on call; we were going to the hospital. He took Ben to my mother's house, which was nearby, and drove me to the emergency room.

There, while Bill was finding a parking space, I encountered the emergency-room triage nurse. I told her that I was in the process of miscarrying. She informed me that I couldn't possibly know that. I explained to her that there had been no heartbeat on the ultrasound on the seventeenth and that the cramping and bleeding that I was experiencing were expected by my physician. She then insisted on asking me questions to which I didn't seem to give the correct answers. After Bill returned and spoke to her, she finally decided that I was deserving of a stretcher, and she assigned me to an examining room.

About an hour later my doctor came in and made arrangements for the D & C. I was wheeled to the holding room in the operating suite. The room had cartoon characters along the ceiling border. I remember thinking that our baby would never know those characters who are so much a part of childhood.

I was wheeled into the operating room, and the next thing I remember is the recovery-room nurse saying my name. I asked her if it was over, and she nodded. It was only at that moment that I first really believed that my baby was dead. Right up until then I had held on to the irrational and unrealistic hope that when the doctor examined me, the baby would somehow be alive and would miraculously survive. My real mourning began at that moment in the recovery room. I cried as silently as I could and waited for my vital signs to stabilize so that I could be with my husband and go home. After a while they gave me my clothes, and a nurse who obviously didn't want to be there ran through a checklist of postoperative instructions. I remember trying to focus on what she was saying but feeling too overwhelmed to process anything. I was glad that Bill was in the room and hoped that he understood what she was saying so that at least one of us would know what to do. I was disappointed that I didn't see my physician after the surgery. Bill said that he had spoken to the doctor in the hall and that he had reported that the procedure went well. Neither of us knew how scraping dead baby parts out of a uterus could go well, but those are the words he chose.

Our life went on with a big empty hole in it. We were forever changed by the death of our child. We never saw him. We never touched him or held him. We don't know what he looked like. We don't even know for sure that he was a boy. But he changed our lives. We appreciate every moment we have together now, because we know that death can knock on any door, at any time.

Most people don't understand our grief. They don't understand how the death of a child whom we never saw can create a painful empty space in our hearts and our family. All I can say is that even though I never held him, I love him with all my heart and miss him more than I could ever have thought possible. It comforts me a little to think of his eternal life, and I look forward to being reunited with him someday in heaven. But, even more, I wish that he could be with me in the here and now.

Amber

Infant Who Died of a Sudden Mysterious Illness

Amber was a happy, healthy baby, the kind of baby parents dream of. She was easygoing, happy-go-lucky, playful, cuddly, and affectionate. She was nine months old and had been cruising around under her own steam for two months. She had started to pull herself up and stand, looking like a little surfboarder as she tried to keep her balance.

The day she got sick, she was happy and playful and had a wonderful time shredding a stack of magazines. I didn't stop her but just watched her enjoying herself as she ripped the colorful pages and squealed with delight. We moved on to other activities as the day unfolded, and a couple of hours later, when I put her on her blanket to change her diaper, she felt a little warm. I took her temperature, and it was 101 degrees. I wasn't too concerned—she was teething, and we were nearing the end of a two-week heat wave that, with the combination of high temperatures and humidity, made it feel like 110 degrees outside. I gave her a dose of Tylenol, fully expecting it to take care of the fever.

About an hour later, I checked her temperature again and was surprised to see that it had gone up to 102.8 degrees. I called the pediatrician's office and reported that Amber was feverish and fussy and that she tired easily after playing for a few minutes. At that point, she showed no signs of dehydration. It was obvious that she didn't feel good and that something was wrong. They made an appointment for her for 3:30 that afternoon. At 1:30, I took her temperature again. It had gone up to 103 degrees. I called work to let them know I wouldn't be coming in (I work evenings, and my husband works nights). I called the doctor's office again, and they said to bring her in right away.

We gathered up our things, fixed her a bottle, and left for the office at around 2:00. By the time we got there, fifteen minutes later, our little girl was completely lethargic and would only take a sip of her juice if it was ice cold. They examined her right away. By now her temperature was 104 degrees. They did blood work and a urinalysis, gave her a dose of Advil, and told us to take her to St. Mary's Hospital immediately.

The twenty-minute ride to the hospital seemed to take much longer. Amber was examined again, and more tests were done. By now she was showing definite signs of dehydration, and IV fluids were started. When they came out of the treatment room, they told me that she had to be transferred downtown to the pediatric intensive care unit of the teaching hospital. St. Mary's PICU was full, and Amber would be transported to the teaching hospital by ambulance and would see an infectious disease specialist there. They said reassuring things about having "caught it early," that things looked good, and that there was a "high percentage" of success. We finally got to see her just before they loaded her into the ambulance. She was not alert. I rode with her in the ambulance and on the elevator to the intensive care unit. In the elevator, I pulled off the face mask they had given me to wear, and when the nurse reprimanded me for it, I replied that I wanted Amber to see my face if she roused enough to open her eyes. I'm so glad I stood my ground, because right after that Amber opened her eyes and looked at me. That was the last time I saw her alive.

Amber died at 1:30 in the morning, while the doctor stepped out to let us know that it didn't look good. She said that every medication and piece of equipment possible was being used to sustain Amber's heartbeat. She asked if we wanted to see her, but when she came back to escort us into the room, I knew by the expression on her face that Amber had died. Our baby died from the effects of meningococcal meningitis just fifteen hours after we discovered that she had a fever of 101 degrees but no other symptoms. We will never know for sure how she contracted it, although the doctors say it was most likely from someone who had intimate contact with her (since she was not in day care, that means me, her dad, or my mother). We later discovered that six out of ten people have the bacteria in their mucous membranes, but it is inactive. If it becomes active (and they don't know how or why it becomes active), that person can infect others, although the carrier may never be affected. There is no test to confirm which people are carriers. Our sweet baby was killed so abruptly by a bacteria that could have come from a simple loving kiss.

Kim

Teenager Killed in a Car Accident

She was a five-foot-two-inch blond—a blue-eyed
ball of fire with an attitude. She didn't back down
for anybody, an attitude that caused a lot of
fireworks. She could also bat those baby blues and
wrap just about anybody around her little finger
in a heartbeat. She loved balloons and Christmas.
Her favorite color was purple.

We were just starting to become very close friends.
She was finally moving out of her rebellious period
and beginning to appreciate the loving care of her
family. We had been through some rough times
together in the past. She was no angel, but none
of us is perfect—we all have our faults. She had
resented the rules that we enforced in our house
(I don't back down, either) and had moved in with
her dad for a while, where she felt she had more
freedom. Her father was never home, and after

some time and many conversations with her friends, she decided to move back in with us.

Kim was really coming around. Our relationship had improved immensely. We had become real friends, and we both enjoyed our daily conversations with each other. I was looking forward to her return home, and I think she was, too.

One Thursday afternoon, she and her cousin went out to get pizza. They were the same age and had been close ever since they were babies. It was one of the few times that Kim rode with someone else. She preferred to drive than to be a passenger. Her cousin was driving much too fast; the car left the road, became airborne, and slammed into a tree on Kim's side. She died from the injuries and never came home again. I lost my daughter and my dear friend.

Randy and Stevie

Teenagers Taken by an Unknown Condition

Randy was my baby and the apple of my eye. He was growing up so well—already seventeen and working at his first real job, bagging groceries and taking them out to customers' cars. He was strong and healthy and smiled easily. He had always been athletic, and the job suited him well. Randy was in the parking lot at work, transferring groceries from the cart to a customer's car, when he just turned blue and collapsed. He was dead before he hit the ground. We didn't know why or how. Neither drugs nor alcohol were involved. My healthy, active teenaged son was just dead. We were devastated and thought that life couldn't get worse.

We moved to the country to get away from some of the memories in our house. We bought horses and found that working with these gentle animals was helpful and healing. Our oldest son, Stevie, seemed to find great peace and consolation in the horses. We all wore Holter monitors for a time to help the doctors try to figure out what had happened to Randy and to determine if any of the rest of us had the same problem.

One day my husband, Steve, left the house to go to work and found Stevie lying dead in the driveway with his car door open and the motor running. Steve immediately began to give Stevie mouth-to-mouth resuscitation but was torn between continuing and calling 911 for help. After some time he finally came in, and we made the call, but it was clear that Stevie had been dead even before Steve found him.

A determination was finally made. Our boys died of cardiomyopathy, a thickening of the heart muscle that results in the loss of the elasticity of the muscle. The heart becomes weaker and weaker until it just stops. Randy and Stevie had a particularly aggressive form of the disease. Since their deaths, Steve has been diagnosed with a less aggressive form. He has also been plagued with colon cancer and severe depression. I have had breast cancer and panic attacks. Our marriage nearly came to an abrupt and painful end. People do strange and hurtful things to try to avoid facing the pain of a child's death: drinking, taking drugs, spending excessively, having love affairs. I won't go into the details regarding our marriage, but it was a mess. Our daughter is a drug addict who, after multiple attempts at therapy and treatment, chose cocaine over her husband and two children. I have done all that I can for her, but still she chooses cocaine.

I have learned that life can get worse after the death of a child. I have survived, but it hasn't been easy. There have been times when I have wished I didn't have to survive. I never knew there could be so much pain in one lifetime—but still we go on. I think I have a better sense now of what is really important. I get aggravated with people who get upset and complain about little things that go wrong. I used to work with a lady whose day was ruined if she broke a nail. I had very little patience with her and often wanted to scream at her and shake her. I have learned to be thankful for the little things that go right. Some days, they are all I have to hold on to.

Matthew

Teenager Felled by Muscular Dystrophy

Matthew was the computer expert in our house. He enjoyed adventure games in which he was able to be the action figure. On the computer it didn't matter that he was in a wheelchair; he could be the ninja, leaping and jumping with amazing agility and grace and brandishing a heavy sword with precision. He was an avid reader of science fiction. Although he wouldn't sing in public, he loved music and sang along with the radio on his computer, which he had programmed with his own musical selections. He was shy in high school, like his mother. He developed an interest in girls a little later than many of his peers. His condition afforded him less independence than other kids his age had. He was naive about many things and as a result had a charming innocence about him. Matthew was extremely intelligent and often surprised others with the depth of his comments.

When Matthew was three and a half or four, he had his own special way of running that was a little different from the way other kids at day care ran. He couldn't get up any speed when he ran. He didn't like to draw or color or play with puzzles. He avoided tasks that required fine motor skills. He preferred playing with trucks and blocks and doing other activities that involved gross motor skills. Although he had begun to walk at the expected time, we thought that perhaps he was a little developmentally delayed or maybe had some kind of learning disability. Testing revealed that Matthew's difficulties were not developmental but neurological. My husband, Jerry, and I are both nurses, and before any diagnosis was formally made, we delved into our textbooks, put our heads together, and figured out that Matthew had Duchenne's muscular dystrophy.

Muscular dystrophy is a neuromuscular disease that progresses slowly and results in muscle weakness that usually affects the legs first and then progresses to all of the muscle systems of the body. Matthew's disease followed the expected course. When he was eight or nine, he began prednisone therapy in an attempt to keep him walking longer. Later, he underwent surgery on the cords and tendons of his feet and legs, also to allow him to walk longer. Recovery was difficult, with long casts on both legs from October to December, followed by long locking leg braces and intense physical therapy. Eventually, of course, the muscles of his legs just couldn't do their job, and before Matthew was in middle school he was using a wheelchair. He enjoyed attending an MDA (Muscular Dystrophy Association) camp every summer, where he developed enduring friendships with counselors and other campers.

By the time Matthew graduated from high school, his scoliosis of the spine had developed to the point that he required major surgery. By then, his lung capacity was down to about a third of what is normal, making surgery very dangerous, with a potential result of Matthew having to spend the rest of his life on a respirator. Luckily, Matthew's lungs tolerated the surgery very well. He was fortunate not to develop the typical complication of pneumonia that so many people with MD acquire. Matthew was able to attend college, and I acted as his aide, transporting him to classes and taking notes for him.

Matthew's final illness was a result of a gradual buildup of carbon dioxide in his system, a complication that results from the inability of muscular dystrophy patients to breathe deeply and efficiently. On a Saturday afternoon we took him to the emergency room, where he fell into a coma. On Sunday we were given a little miracle. Matthew woke up and recognized me. This should have been impossible with the level of carbon dioxide in his system. He was lucid and responsive for a couple of hours. He enjoyed playing briefly with our little dog, Bullet, and said, "I love you, Mommy" and spoke to his grandmother on the phone. Even after he was no longer alert, Matthew knew that we were standing on either side of his bed. He looked back and forth from me to his dad in response to our voices. Matthew died peacefully on Monday, October 23. He was nineteen years old. We won't be taking him to camp this Father's Day weekend. What will we do without him?

Alecia

Sister Killed Violently during a Random Crime

My sister Alecia was a sophomore at an urban college about a hundred miles from home. Mom and Dad couldn't understand why she had picked that school over the quiet rural campus that was her second choice, but she loved the hubbub of the city and was stimulated and exhilarated by the action and diversity of big-city life.

Alecia and her roommate had taken their clothes to the Laundromat. After they filled their machines, Alecia left to get drinks, snacks, and more change at the convenience store around the corner. Before she reached the checkout, a gunman came in to rob the place. He terrorized everyone in the store for a while, then killed the young clerk and Alecia before leaving with $287. According to witnesses and the security videotape, neither of them did anything to provoke the thief. He simply shot them.

I don't know how to make sense of any of it. I have nightmares full of fear and violence and blood. I don't want to remember my sister that way. She was so sweet and funny, so full of life. How can she be dead? I don't know how to live the rest of my life without her.

Ricky

Teenager Killed by Drunk Driving

It had been a tough couple of years for Ricky.
In spite of our trying to keep things as amiable as
possible, the divorce had been messy and was
difficult on all of us. I know he felt abandoned by
his father (I did, too). It's especially hard for a
young kid to have to go through something like
that. He was only fourteen when his dad
announced that he was leaving. Just when he
needed his dad the most he was stuck with me.
His big brother had recently left for college, and
his little sister was too young to be of any real help
to him.

By the time Ricky started high school, we had begun
to get into a routine and to be comfortable with
our new life together. About halfway into the
new school year he began to hang out with some
different kids. They were a little rougher, and I

wasn't as comfortable with them. He started dressing differently and testing his limits more. I knew the teen years were supposed to be a time of rebellion, and I tried to be patient and diligent at the same time. Ricky resented having to tell me where he was going and who he was with all the time. He sulked and whined and complained about his curfew. He started to talk about wanting to live with his father instead of me. We were fighting more and more.

I tried to help him understand that I was being strict because I loved him. He thought I didn't trust him. I was worried that he would become openly defiant or belligerent, because I honestly didn't know how I would handle that. I was trying to think of solutions and strategies to implement if things escalated between us, but it never got to that point.

One Saturday night Ricky went with his friends to a party where people were drinking. It was still early when a group of kids from the party climbed into a car. A boy who had just gotten his license took them for a spin, lost control on a curve, and sailed off the road and into a tree-lined ravine. Ricky was in the backseat and died before the paramedics could get him out of the car. I feel so guilty. I shouldn't have let him go out that night.

~ BAD NEWS

[T]hey have heard bad news;
they melt in fear, they are troubled like the sea
that cannot be quiet.

JEREMIAH 49:23

DREAD

Whaen I opened the
door and saw the uniformed officer, I knew right
away that something terrible had happened. I was
immediately filled with dread and foreboding,
but of course his news was more horrible than
anything I could have imagined. It was a blow of
enormous proportions. I wanted to do something,
to go somewhere to help my children, but there
was nothing I could do to help. It didn't seem
real. It still doesn't.

Dread came upon me, and trembling,

which made all my bones shake.

JOB 4:14

She was bright and beautiful, vivacious and friendly, kind and sincere. Her health was important to her. She ate well (remarkably well for a teenager), got plenty of exercise, and avoided drugs and the people who did them. She worked hard, studied hard, and played hard. She loved her family and was close to God. She should have had a long and happy life. It was just an accident. It was nobody's fault. It just happened, and my beautiful little girl is gone.

~ 48

Again I saw that under the sun the race is not to the swift, nor the battle to the strong, nor bread to the wise, nor riches to the intelligent, nor favor to the skillful; but time and chance happen to them all.

ECCLESIASTES 9:11

49 ~

SUDDEN CHANGE

*H*ow quickly our lives changed. Our boy was growing so well. We loved him and were proud of him. He was a good boy. He would have been a teenager soon. He was looking forward to that. The doctor said that his heart just stopped beating during football practice. He loved football.

For you yourselves know very well that the day of the Lord will come like a thief in the night.

1 THESSALONIANS 5:2

BAD NEWS

I don't really understand what happened. Nobody will explain it to me. The police came. Mom and Dad told me that she was dead, but nobody told me much of anything else. I guess they think I won't understand. She was my sister. I want to know what happened to her. Not knowing makes me more scared. I feel left out of the family, and I keep imagining all kinds of terrible things. I wish they would talk to me. It makes me angry that they think I'm not grown-up enough for them to tell me what happened to my sister. Everybody talks to me like I'm a baby, or they stop talking, or they change the way they talk when I'm around. It's really insulting.

Even when I cry out, "Violence!" I am not answered;

I call aloud, but there is no justice.

*S*eeing him in such pain was so dreadful. He bore it bravely and with little complaint, but how I wished that the pain could have been given to me instead of him. Knowing that he would have no more pain made it a little easier to let him go. I'm glad that he is no longer in pain, but I miss him very much.

~ 54

He will wipe every tear from their eyes.

Death will be no more;

mourning and crying and pain will be no more.

REVELATION 21:4

*E*very time I close my
eyes I see her limp, lifeless body floating in the
water. I try not to think of her disoriented and
panicking, desperate for air; or gasping and
thrashing and finally overcome by the force of the
water. I try not to think of her pale, bluish, waxy-
looking skin, of her hollow eyes, or of how very
cold she was. This is not how I want to remember
my warm and vibrant daughter. I don't know how
to banish these dreadful images. I try not to see
them. I try to think of other things, to see other
images; instead these come to mind unbidden
and unwanted.

~ 56

I have great sorrow and unceasing anguish in my heart.

*T*he dreaded phone call finally came. Shocking, but not completely unexpected. He had chosen a life fraught with danger and self-destruction. We tried everything: counseling, bailing him out of trouble time and again, more counseling, treatment, behavior modification, more treatment, tough love, and, through it all, constant prayers. We have always loved him and tried to be there for him when he needed us. He knew he had a loving home to come to, but he preferred the company of his companions—I won't call them friends, because they were not interested in what was best for him. I had such hope the last time I saw him. He seemed more open and more willing to see the effects of his choices. He had been clean for more than four months. I remember thinking

~ 58

that maybe he was finally growing up a little and
starting to be more responsible. Even though
he had been so far away for so many years, he
had been close to my heart and in my prayers
every moment of every day. I can't believe he is
really dead.

Can a mother forget her infant,

  be without tenderness for the child of her womb?

Isaiah 49:15 (NAB)

*M*y dad used to always pray for a peaceful death. I never really understood that prayer until now. I figured that death is death. What difference does it make how you die?

~ 60

I keep thinking about how scared she must have been just before she died, surrounded by terror and violence and evil. I wish I could have been there in her place. If she had to die, I wish it could have been peacefully, with time to reflect and prepare, and with her family by her side.

I have taken up my father's prayer for all of us.

As for yourself, you shall go to your ancestors in peace; you shall be buried in a good old age.

GENESIS 15:15

THE FIRE

*T*here was some kind of short in the heating system under our floorboards. The fire started in the middle of the night when we were all sleeping. We woke up when the fire burned part of the wiring to the doorbell, making it ring continuously. By then the smoke was thick. Her room was closest to the fire. I could feel the heat and hear a crackling sound as I walked across her floor. I thought she was sleeping when I carried her outside, but she never woke up. Later the fire chief told me that it was the smoke that killed her. He said that it was a miracle the rest of us got out alive. Another ten or fifteen minutes and all of us would have been dead. I am grateful for our lives, but I wish the doorbell had started ringing just a few minutes earlier so that she could have lived, too.

When you walk through fire you shall not be burned,

   and the flame shall not consume you.

For I am the LORD your God.

ISAIAH 43:2—3

I am angry. I am angry at
that boy who was speeding. I am angry at myself for
not protecting her better. I am angry at her for
not wearing her seat belt and for dying. I am angry
at the highway department for not putting a stop-
light at that intersection. I am angry at God for
taking my child from me and not protecting her.
You know how I love her. I thought you loved me
too much to let this happen, God.

~ 64

Be angry but do not sin; do not let the sun go down on your anger, and do not make room for the devil.

EPHESIANS 4:26—27

65 ~

*I*t was two weeks after school let out for the summer. Grandma and Grandpa took our four kids fishing on their boat, as they had many times before. The kids loved their special time with Gramps and Nana and looked forward to every chance they had to get out on the boat. It was just a day trip. We packed picnic baskets and coolers and coated everybody with sunscreen. There was a terrible boating accident. None of the children survived. I hate summer.

Like water my life drains away;
　all my bones grow soft.
My heart has become like wax,
　it melts away within me.
As dry as a potsherd is my throat;
　my tongue sticks to my palate;
　you lay me in the dust of death.

PSALM 22:15–16 (NAB)

GUILTY

*E*veryone says it was an accident, and it was—but I was there. I should have been able to protect her. I should have been able to save her. That is what parents are supposed to do. I feel so guilty, so full of shame, so worthless.

~ 68

Do not give yourself over to sorrow,

and do not distress yourself deliberately.

SIRACH 30:21

69 ~

*T*he very word conjures images of darkness and horror and shame. When it applies to your own child it means being overcome by guilt, remorse, and an endless list of unanswered questions. My darling, I miss you so. Didn't you know how much I love you?

~ 70

They despair of returning from darkness.

JOB 15:22

*T*he police officer was so kind. He came by one day when he was off duty and told us that our son had died in his arms. This man had done all he could to help our son, but the injuries were too great. Our son was dead before the paramedics arrived. The officer told us that he prayed over our son as he held him and that our son didn't suffer. The officer hugged us before he left, and I was glad that the strong arms of that kind man had held our son at the end. I wouldn't have wanted him to be alone.

I am going to send an angel in front of you, to guard you on the way and to bring you to the place that I have prepared.

EXODUS 23:20

BAD NEWS

~ EARLY GRIEF

There is anger and envy and trouble and unrest,
*   and fear of death, and fury and strife.*
And when one rests upon his bed,
*   his sleep at night confuses his mind.*

SIRACH 40:5

I always knew in an intellectual sense that death is a fact of life. But with the death of my child that fact has hit me right between the eyes, and it is no soft blow. Now death permeates every corner of my life and seeps into every crack. I had no idea what life really was before now. I didn't know it could be so sad. I don't think I'll ever be really happy again.

~ 76

You have made known to me the ways of life;

you will make me full of gladness with your presence.

ACTS 2:28

77 ~

I feel so tired, so drained of every drop of energy and hope. I feel empty and sad and exhausted. I just want everybody to leave me alone. I can't make any more decisions. I can't talk to even one more person. I just want to curl up in a dark corner with a blanket over my head and have the rest of the world forget about me and leave me alone. I don't even have the strength to grieve.

~ 78

I will satisfy the weary,

and all who are faint I will replenish.

JEREMIAH 31:25

Quarrelsome

I feel so guilty. Our last words were not pleasant ones. We argued again that last day. I will always regret that we parted with tension and anger that morning. We were both running late and planned to resume our discussion later in the day. I thought it was an important issue at the time. I wish that, instead of quarreling, I had touched him and told him that I loved him.

And the Lord's servant must not be quarrelsome but

kindly to everyone, an apt teacher, patient.

2 TIMOTHY 2:24

I can't talk about my child's death. It doesn't comfort or reassure me. It only hurts more to talk about it. Talking seems to help my wife, but it only brings me pain. I can't talk about it, but I haven't forgotten anything. Each detail of his too-short life is etched in my memory and will always be in my heart. But don't make me talk about it. Not now.

His memory is as sweet as honey to every mouth,

and like music at a banquet of wine.

SIRACH 49:1

*F*or me, solitude helps. When I am alone and busy with something that occupies my hands, I am more at peace. I can't be around people hugging and crying and talking right now. My child is dead. I don't want to talk about it. I want to be left alone, to find my own peace.

It seems to help my wife to have people around to hug, to cry with, and to talk to, over and over again. That makes me crazy. I can't stand it.

I went to the basement and organized my workbench. I found a place for everything and put it all away. Alone in the basement I could think and pray, and I could accomplish something. As a result of that time alone, I am more at peace than I have been at any time since he died.

Help her to understand, God, that although I love her and need her, right now I just need some time to myself.

Woman is not independent of man or man independent of woman. For just as woman came from man, so man comes through woman; but all things come from God.

1 CORINTHIANS 11:11–12

UNCLE JOE

*T*he kids are always glad to see their Uncle Joe when he stops by. He has a quiet way of making everybody feel better. He's a big help to me, too. He gives me good hugs, but mostly he takes care of practical details—things that need doing that I just can't deal with or haven't even noticed. Often he says some little thing that makes me laugh, and he never lets me take myself too seriously. He gives me comfort by being himself—my big brother.

A friend loves at all times,

   and kinsfolk are born to share adversity.

PROVERBS 17:17

I still wake up with the sounds of the accident in my ears and can see it all again in the flashes of my dreams. It is scary and horrible, but at least during the nightmares, for a little while, she is still alive.

~ 88

You heard my plea, "Do not close your ear

to my cry for help, but give me relief!"

LAMENTATIONS 3:56

*P*eople try to be comfort-
ing. They don't know how. "It's for the best," they
say. "God wanted her with him." As if God were a
selfish ogre who delights in our misery. They say
other dumb things, too, that hurt much more than
they help: "You're young, you can have another,"
as if one child could replace another, or "You
should be getting over this by now." The thoughtless
comments are legion and unbelievable, but I do
my best to grit my teeth and bite my tongue. I try
to remind myself that these people are trying to
be helpful.

I wish I could let people know that anything that
diminishes or discounts our loss is hurtful rather
than helpful. It's better to express sympathy with a
look or a touch than to say some stupid thing to

"cheer up" a grieving parent or sibling. We don't need cheering up. We need friends who will acknowledge our loss and sympathize with us.

Help me to see only their loving concern for me, Lord, and to draw from you the comfort that they can't give.

They shall obtain joy and gladness,
and sorrow and sighing shall flee away.

I, I am he who comforts you.

Isaiah 51:11–12

~ 92

I often find that I must
actively will myself to relax the muscles of my body.
I will be sitting, doing nothing in particular—like
watching television or reading the paper—and I
will realize that all my muscles are tense and tight,
as if I am poised to run or attack. My body is rigid
and waiting—waiting for I don't know what. I take
some deep breaths and try to relax my muscles, but
a little while later I discover that they are taut
and strained again. I am trembling and shivering,
my bones are shaking, and the muscle tension
must be adding to my fatigue. I don't know how to
relax.

Be gracious to me, O Lord, for I am languishing;

O Lord, heal me, for my bones are shaking

with terror.

PSALM 6:2

I seem to constantly remember every detail of her brief life. Yesterday I was thinking about when I first discovered I was pregnant with her (how happy we were!) and how excited I was the first time I felt her move within me. She was such a delight from the very beginning. How can I live without her? It's like all that is bright and good and beautiful has been swept out of the world. Help me to see the other miracles around me. I feel like the world has changed from Technicolor to black and white.

~ 94

In those days Mary set out and went with haste to a Judean town in the hill country, where she entered the house of Zechariah and greeted Elizabeth. When Elizabeth heard Mary's greeting, the child leaped in her womb. And Elizabeth was filled with the Holy Spirit and exclaimed with a loud cry, "Blessed are you among women, and blessed is the fruit of your womb."

LUKE 1:39–42

*T*here seemed to be so many people at the funeral. The whole family was there, along with many friends. There were a lot of people I didn't know, her friends from school and sports and work whom I had never met. It was a great tribute to her and a wonderful support to us. It helps to be reminded of how many people love and care for us. Our friends and family are such a comfort.

~ 96

Do not fear, for I am with you;

I will bring your offspring from the east,

and from the west I will gather you;

I will say to the north, "Give them up,"

and to the south, "Do not withhold;

bring my sons from far away

and my daughters from the end of the earth."

Isaiah 43:5–6

GOD'S WILL

*I*t is God's will," people say. I just can't reconcile that statement with a child's death. They don't go together. God wills life, sunshine, and gentle breezes. God wills majestic mountains and fields of wildflowers. God wills satisfying sex and melodious music. God wills family harmony and joyous celebration. God wills exuberant praise, abundant thanksgiving, and heartfelt petition. God does not will death, destruction, and disease.

So it is not the will of your Father in heaven that one of these little ones should be lost.

MATTHEW 18:14

My poor children—I know that they are not getting the attention and care they need and deserve. I try not to neglect them, but right now I don't seem to have the strength, energy, or concentration to do more than meet their most basic needs. They have had to fix their own breakfast almost every day this week. I don't think they have any clean socks to wear. There is no milk in the house (I've been to the store twice but forgot to buy milk both times). I want to hold them close and fulfill their every need and take away their pain. I am a failure at everything.

"So have no fear; I myself will provide for you and your little ones." In this way he reassured them, speaking kindly to them.

GENESIS 50:21

*A*s I look back over the recent past, I realize that I have been practically sleepwalking through my life in a blur of pain and numbness. Maybe the fact that I realize it now means that I am beginning to pass through it. I feel as though a big part of me died with my child. It seems to have been the happy part. Will I ever be happy again?

It is now the moment for you to wake from sleep. For salvation is nearer to us now than when we became believers; the night is far gone, the day is near.

Romans 13:11–12

I need time alone now as I never have before. I need time to allow myself to cry and hurt and remember. It is painful, but I know I need it. Sometimes I take out pictures to look at and things to touch that I know will bring out very strong feelings and memories. I find times to do this when Mom and Dad aren't home. I think the intensity of my grief would upset them, or they might try to comfort me or tell me to stop or say that "everything will be all right." They are hurting and grieving, too, but I believe it would hurt them even more to see me hurting so much. So I try to wait for my special time when I can be alone so that they won't have to worry so much about me. It seems odd to hide my grief in a loving family, but it is because we love one another and want to spare one another additional pain. I wonder if they have their own special time when they grieve more than they let me see. I wonder why we can't do it together.

With that, Joseph hurried out, because he was overcome with affection for his brother, and he was about to weep. So he went into a private room and wept there.

GENESIS 43:30

*I*t's hard to concentrate on my schoolwork. Even the subjects that used to be easy are really hard now. I am always forgetting what I am trying to do. I can't keep my mind on what I am doing. The other day the teacher called on me, and I didn't know what she was talking about. It wouldn't have been so bad except that I thought I was paying attention. Homework is even worse. I can't seem to get anything done at home. I feel so sad, knowing that she isn't there and that she's not coming home.

Do not fear, for I am with you,

    do not be afraid, for I am your God;

I will strengthen you, I will help you,

    I will uphold you with my victorious right hand.

ISAIAH 41:10

EARLY GRIEF

THE SMELL OF HIM

I remember the smell of his baby-soft skin: warm milk, baby powder, and soap. Later, when he was big enough to dig in the flower beds and play on the swings, he smelled of dirt and dust and a child's sweet perspiration. As a teenager he worked hard and played hard and would come in sweaty and dirty, smelling like a locker room. His first job was cutting grass, and he would come home smelling of grass clippings and gasoline. He loved to come in and give me a big bear hug to tease me. I would push him away and tell him to go take a shower, but I made sure I got a good hug first.

I still remember how he reeked of his dad's aftershave when he went on his first real date. In college he worked late nights in a restaurant and couldn't wait to get out of his clothes when he came home. Grease and cigarette smells went right into the washer.

But mostly I remember how he smelled when we sat together watching TV: a warm, clean, manly smell that was my son.

Ah, the smell of my son
   is like the smell of a field that the LORD has blessed.   109 ~
May God give you of the dew of heaven,
   and of the fatness of the earth,
   and plenty of grain and wine.

GENESIS 27:27–28

THE PILE OF BOXES

*W*hen everything was
packed up, it seemed to be such a small, sad pile
of boxes. The collection of clothes and toys seemed
too small to represent her whole short life with
us. We saved a few special things, but the sum of
her existence was so much greater than the sum
of her possessions.

Are not two sparrows sold for a penny? Yet not one of them will fall to the ground apart from your Father.

MATTHEW 10:29

III ~

EARLY GRIEF

~ QUESTIONING

O my God, I cry by day, but you do not answer;
   and by night, but find no rest.

PSALM 22:2

But when I look there is no one;
   among these there is no counselor
   who, when I ask, gives an answer.

ISAIAH 41:28

I don't understand. How can this be? I thought it was a simple illness. How can a strong and healthy child die of a simple illness in this day and age? They said there were "complications" and things that "couldn't be prevented." How can my child be dead? What happened? How did it happen? I don't understand.

Just as you do not know how the breath comes to the bones in the mother's womb, so you do not know the work of God, who makes everything.

ECCLESIASTES 11:5

QUESTIONING

HOSPITAL BED

*I*t was so scary seeing her lying still and pale in the hospital bed. She looked so small and vulnerable. There were so many tubes and wires and machines and monitors. I looked at the machines and tried to make some sense of the lights and numbers and squiggles and beeps. Everything seemed to be going fine. At first it was a little touch and go, but then they said she had stabilized. How could she have died? I don't understand the sense of it or the science of it. I only know that my little girl is gone. Why didn't you heal her, God?

Is there no balm in Gilead?

Is there no physician there?

JEREMIAH 8:22

QUESTIONING

Υou smile up at me from the picture on top of my desk. How I miss that smile. I wonder if you really knew how that grin melted my heart. When you were very little you used to run, grinning, to meet me at the door, outstretching your chubby little arms so that I could pick you up. No greeting was more wonderful. As you got older you would grin with delight, throw your curls back, and laugh when something struck your funny bone. There were quiet smiles of reassurance, encouragement, and support that you gave me like a secret signal over the years. There were smirks of mischief and conspiratory giggles as we plotted together to surprise someone else. Most often there was the quiet smile of contentment that defined you. Your eyes lit up whenever you smiled. I knew how special your smiles were, and

I made a point to take pictures in my mind so that I would have your smiles as cherished memories. I thought I would take so many more as you grew up and away and into your own life. My collection of smile "pictures" is not nearly large enough. How can I continue for the rest of my life without being able to add to it?

I smiled on them when they had no confidence;

and the light of my countenance they did

not extinguish.

JOB 29:24

QUESTIONING

I don't understand. How can this be? How can my precious child be dead? Why did this happen? I can find no answers. I don't know where to turn. I don't know what to do. My whole life has changed. I feel like I am standing alone asking questions that no one hears. The world rushes by, and no one answers me. To other people my questions are meaningless, but to me they mean everything. Even God is not listening. I can no longer make sense of my life. I no longer know how to live.

I cry to you and you do not answer me;

I stand, and you merely look at me.

You have turned cruel to me;

with the might of your hand you persecute me.

JOB 30:20—21

~ 122

When my daughter died, my whole life changed. It's as if everything I thought was important and meaningful is now hollow and unimportant. I find myself questioning everything I ever believed. I don't understand why she died or what any of this means. I question the existence and role of God in my life. I don't understand how God could let this happen. My faith used to be strong. I don't know how to get it back.

Why are you cast down, O my soul,

   and why are you disquieted within me?

Hope in God; for I shall again praise him,

   my help and my God.

PSALM 42:11

QUESTIONING

TOMORROW

I can't imagine a tomorrow without her. How can I walk into a future when she has no future? How can tomorrow possibly have meaning without her? I don't want to have a tomorrow anymore. I can't even think about tomorrow. I can barely get through today.

Do not worry about tomorrow; tomorrow will take care of itself. Sufficient for a day is its own evil.

Matthew 6:34 (NAB)

Violence had never really
touched my life before. How could our child have
been murdered? We don't live in the projects.
We live in a good neighborhood. We don't have
anything to do with drugs. Our children don't do
dangerous things. If anything, we have always been
overprotective. This kind of thing happens to other
people, not to people like us. I feel so vulnerable,
surrounded by evil. I used to be so trusting, but
now I fear every stranger I see. Is he the one who
killed my child? True evil was never real to me
before. Now its shadows surround me, and I shake
with fear.

They cried out in fear. But immediately Jesus spoke to them and said, "Take heart, it is I; do not be afraid."

MATTHEW 14:26–27

*I*f only we had understood. If only we had listened. If only we had been there. If only we had stood our ground. If only we had eased up a little. If only we hadn't quarreled. If only we had gone to the doctor sooner. If only . . . We revisit every fact over and over, searching for something we could have or should have done differently, something that might have changed the outcome. We agonize over the smallest detail that we didn't notice or that we forgot or ignored, searching for some reason, some explanation, some understanding, some knowledge of WHY?

Do nothing without deliberation,

but when you have acted, do not regret it.

Do not go on a path full of hazards,

and do not stumble at an obstacle twice.

Sirach 32:19—20

*W*e were really happy—a little crazy, maybe, but we had a lot of fun together. I thanked God every day for our blessings and our wonderful life together. There seem to be so few really happy families, but ours truly was one. Now we are so sad. I can't imagine the rest of my life without him. Will I ever be happy again? Our dreams and hopes disappeared with his death.

Are any among you suffering? They should pray. Are
any cheerful? They should sing songs of praise.

JAMES 5:13

I worry about a lot of things: Will the other children be all right? Can they be safe in this world—can I protect them? Will they be able to get through this emotionally? Will our marriage survive the strain? Where will the money come from for the medical and funeral expenses? How can I adjust to living without my child? I just can't take it all on. I can hardly keep myself going. I have to give it over to you, Lord. All I can do is try to get through a day at a time without doing any more damage to the people I love. Please take care of them, Lord, at least until I can.

I want you to be free from anxieties.

1 CORINTHIANS 7:32

~ 134

I worry about the children. This is such a sad and broken home. None of us is functioning well. All this grief is too much to bear. We are dull and dazed and in pain. We try to comfort one another and show our love and affection for one another as we try to deal with this death, but none of us knows what to do. Is there a right way to grieve? Each of us handles it in a different way. Our emotions are right at the surface. We are easily bruised by the world and by one another. We feel guilty and angry and hurt and sorrowful. We turn inward—yet we lash out. We remember—yet we try to forget. The problem is that although we are each doing these things, we do them at different times and in different ways. I don't think any of us wants to come home to this desolate place, but we don't really want to go out and face the world either. I don't know how to help my children. I don't know how to help myself. I don't know how to grieve. I don't know how to live.

Out of the depths I cry to you, O Lord.

P SALM 130:1

I really thought she would make it. She was young and strong and determined, and the tumor wasn't big. She suffered a lot with the chemotherapy, but we continued to hope, and she fought so hard. In the end it was plain that only hope and prayers were left. Medicine had done all it could. Why weren't hope and prayers enough?

Hope deferred makes the heart sick,
    but a desire fulfilled is a tree of life.

PROVERBS 13:12

MEANIE

I wish I hadn't been so mean to my sister. It drove her crazy. I thought it was fun to tease her, but it really made her mad. I wish that I hadn't teased her so much. I don't think she liked me. I don't know. Maybe she thought I didn't like her because I teased her so much—but I did like her. I loved her. I wish I could tell her how much. Why didn't I ever tell her? Why was I so mean? I hope she understands. I hope she knows that I love her.

Come to me, all you that are weary and are carrying heavy burdens, and I will give you rest.

MATTHEW 11:28

I don't know for sure what I believe anymore. I try to figure out how God could have let this happen to my little sister. Sometimes I don't think God has anything to do with anything. I wonder if there is a God and if he really does care. Other times I am sure that God is there and that everything happens for a reason, or even if there is no reason, that God can help some good come out of horrible things. I don't know which is true. Thinking there is no God makes me feel bitter and angry and mean inside, and very empty. But believing that God loves us, even though this terrible thing happened, makes me feel hopeful. It's hard enough to believe that my sister is dead. I don't want to believe that God is dead, too.

We know that all things work together for good for those who love God, who are called according to his purpose.

ROMANS 8:28

*I*t's your birthday tomorrow, but you won't be here to celebrate—you haven't been for many years. Long ago I passed the birthday that made me older than you will ever be. That was a hard one. After you died, did you stay the child you were, or are we still twenty-seven months apart? When I see you again will you be the way I remember you or the way I think of you now? I don't know, but I will send flowers to Mom and Dad and thank them, and God, for you. You have always been a big part of my life, and always will be. Happy birthday.

~ 142

I thank my God every time I remember you, constantly
praying with joy in every one of my prayers for all of you.

PHILIPPIANS 1:3—4

~ INTO THE PIT

I called on your name, O Lord,
from the depths of the pit.
LAMENTATIONS 3:55

I must be dying. It seems like I should be bleeding. How can anyone feel so bad and still live? How can anyone hurt so badly and not be bleeding somewhere? How can I go on? I don't know how to live or what to do. I move from place to place and room to room but don't remember doing it. Somehow I seem to talk to people, although I don't know what I have said. I am bereft. My heart is broken. My darling is gone.

He heals the brokenhearted,

and binds up their wounds.

PSALM 147:3

147 ~

INTO THE PIT

I feel like one of those people we sometimes see on the news after a tornado has sucked up and destroyed their homes. They stand blinking into the camera, appearing lost and confused as they look around at the place where their homes had stood such a brief time before.

I am lost and confused and feel as though everything has been destroyed. The odd thing is that when I look around me, everything appears the same. My belongings are all here; the furniture is in place; people speak to me in the same way they always have. Nothing has changed at the office. My boss's expectations of me are identical to the ones he had before my child died.

Everything looks the same, but to me it's hollow and meaningless. Nobody seems to realize that nothing is the same. My whole world is gone. It seems as if I am in a *Twilight Zone* episode where I have been transported to an alternate dimension and no one there recognizes that this life is not the real one. It is as if I am living in a mirror and everything is flat and meaningless. I want to get out of the mirror and back to my real life, but no one will help me or even let me. They don't realize that there is a problem. They can't comprehend that my real life has been stolen from me.

Enemies have stretched out their hands
   over all her precious things;
she has even seen the nations
   invade her sanctuary.

LAMENTATIONS 1:10

*S*ometimes I wonder if Mama and Daddy will ever love me as much as they love my brother. If I were the one who had died, would they miss me as much as they miss him? I don't really think so. He was so special and so good. They are always talking about him or purposely *not* talking about him. I know that they are always thinking of him. I can tell by their faces, and I also know because I am always thinking of him, too.

~ 150

I have great sorrow and unceasing anguish in my heart.

ROMANS 9:2

*S*omehow I get through the days, plodding through one task after another, but the nights drag on endlessly. Sleep comes fitfully and only after hours of too much thinking and crying and lying awake missing you. I am flooded with memories and with dreams of a future for you that will never come to be. How can you be gone? How can life be so empty and painful and still go on?

I have been assigned months of misery,

    and troubled nights have been told off for me.

JOB 7:3 (NAB)

I think about her all the time and miss her so much. When I'm in a room and feeling lonely without her, I try to tell myself that it is almost like it was when she used to just be in her room or somewhere in the neighborhood, doing something—but it's not the same at all. Sometimes at night when I can't sleep, I lie on her bed and look at her picture. I feel close to her there with my head on her pillow. I cry and cry, and sometimes I feel a little better.

They wail upon their beds.

HOSEA 7:14

INTO THE PIT

I don't know what you expect of me, God. This is too much to bear. I do not have the strength for this burden. I struggle under the weight of my grief, my memories, and my hopelessness.

~ 156

Is my strength the strength of stones,

   or is my flesh bronze?

JOB 6:12

INTO THE PIT

~ 158

I am so afraid. Now I know that terrible things don't just happen to other people. The violence of my child's death has made me feel weak and vulnerable. I am finding every aspect of my life almost impossible. I can't concentrate at work. I'm afraid that I might lose my job. My family is devastated. We don't know how to comfort one another. I can see no end to this pain and misery. I'm afraid that I am falling apart and that my whole life is crumbling before my eyes. I'm terrified that somebody will notice that this is all a facade and that I am just going through the motions of life. When that happens, everything will really fall apart.

We look for peace, but find no good,

    for a time of healing, but there is terror instead.

JEREMIAH 8:15

I think I am going crazy. Sometimes I just start crying and sobbing for no reason. I can't seem to control it. Other times I get so angry that I just want to scream and hit people and break things. I can't seem to concentrate on things around me. I keep forgetting important things, and I lose everything. I don't want to say anything about it to my parents. That's all they need now, on top of everything else—a crazy kid. I don't know what to do, so I just keep pretending to be fine.

Cast all your anxiety on him, because he cares for you.

1 PETER 5:7

INTO THE PIT

I force myself to eat, but it's not easy. I'm never hungry, and food seems to stick in my throat. I used to enjoy eating, but now I'm losing weight, and I don't even care. I used to want to lose weight. I used to love to cook. Now it's all kind of repulsive.

~ 162

Therefore, we are not discouraged; rather, although our outer self is wasting away, our inner self is being renewed day by day.

2 CORINTHIANS 4:16 (NAB)

*M*y treasure is gone. My daughter is dead. She was the brightest, most wonderful thing in my life. She grew lovelier every day, and her love for me never wavered, to my continued amazement. Even when she was a teenager she and I were still close, and she confided many things to her old dad. I have always been so proud of her. She had become a wonderful young woman. I am bereft. She was my greatest wealth and all that really mattered.

Do not be afraid, my son, because we have become poor. You have great wealth if you fear God and flee from every sin and do what is good in the sight of the Lord your God.

TOBIT 4:21

I guess I've lived my life in a little bubble of peace and happiness. I have been blessed with so many things: a loving family, a happy childhood, a good education, a fulfilling job, a devoted spouse, good health, strong faith, and the best daughter in the world. We had our ups and downs, but all in all we had a happy existence. Now the bubble has been burst, and I see the evil and ugliness around me. I feel so vulnerable and afraid. My world has been invaded by death and destruction, and all my protection is gone.

She was so bright and talented—the crowning glory of my life. I had so many grand hopes for her future and so many plans for her happiness.

My soul is bereft of peace;

    I have forgotten what happiness is;

so I say, "Gone is my glory,

    and all that I had hoped for from the LORD."

SHE DOESN'T NOTICE

*B*efore my brother died, my mother always seemed to notice when something was wrong with me. She would rub my back and ask me if I wanted to talk about it. Sometimes she would make me go with her on errands, just so she could be alone with me in the car to ask me what was wrong. Now she doesn't notice. I understand. It's probably my fault, too, because now I try to hide it when something is wrong. But still, I wish she would notice.

Look on my right hand and see—

   there is no one who takes notice of me;

no refuge remains to me;

   no one cares for me.

PSALM 142:4

I never knew a person could cry so much. The tears just keep coming. Sometimes I know that something will make me cry, like holding something of my brother's or thinking about something that we did together before he died. Other times I am completely surprised when I start crying. It seems to be for no reason. Mostly it is because something reminds me of him when I don't expect it to. But little things also seem to hurt my feelings or make me feel angry, and I will cry then, too. I feel like such a crybaby, but I can't seem to stop the tears.

My eyes will flow without ceasing,

without respite.

LAMENTATIONS 3:49

171 ~

*W*e used to be so busy. We shuttled between work and home and school and gulped down our hurried dinner to dash off to soccer or Scouts or basketball or PTA meetings or music lessons or church events. We ran to get milk and bread for breakfast and poster board for last-minute projects. Now we sit over our silent supper, hearing the clock tick and having no place to go. I look in your eyes and see the pain in your soul that matches mine. How long will it be before we are able to make a new life alone together?

How long, O LORD? Will you forget me forever?
  How long will you hide your face from me?
How long must I bear pain in my soul,
  and have sorrow in my heart all day long?

*W*ill this suffering never end? The pain of my little girl's death is so intense. I am incapable of functioning in any real way. I can't move. I can't work. I can't eat. Everything hurts too much. My thoughts torture me. My hopes and dreams are shattered. My memories are too few, and my life no longer has meaning or purpose. I don't know how I can ever be better. All I can do is cry. Sleep is my only relief, and it is elusive.

~ 174

I am weary with my moaning;

every night I flood my bed with tears;

I drench my couch with my weeping.

PSALM 6:6

~ 176

*W*e hear our parents say that we are "so resilient," that we are "adapting" and "adjusting" well. Can't they hear us screaming inside? Don't they know that we are pretending to be well for their sake? We have to adjust our reactions to what we think they can handle. We're always testing their reactions by being a little bit truthful and then pulling back if they're not ready. They think we are less affected than they are by our brother's death, but we are only acting this way to protect our parents. Maybe soon they will be better and we can let them know how we really feel.

Thus says the LORD:
We have heard a cry of panic,
  of terror, and no peace.

JEREMIAH 30:5

177 ~

INTO THE PIT

We feel so lonely, God. She was full of life and brought such sparkle—and yes, often fireworks—into our lives. Everything is dull and dim without her. We didn't always get along with her, but we always loved her intensely. How can she be gone? We weren't finished fighting!

~ 178

I will not leave you orphaned; I am coming to you.

JOHN 14:18

I feel so sad and lonely and empty inside. Nothing excites me or cheers me up anymore. The things that used to mean so much seem stupid and meaningless now. I don't know how to get better. I don't know how to be happy again. The people I used to turn to can't help me. They feel the same way I do. Will I ever get better? Will my life always be this dark and scary? Does anybody know how to help me?

I go about in sunless gloom;

I stand up in the assembly and cry for help.

JOB 30:28

I didn't just lose my sister. When she died, my family died, too. I know now that our family will never be the same again. A part of me died, too, the carefree part that didn't worry about bad things happening or families changing. I guess my childhood ended. I don't want to grow up this way. I want to be a lighthearted kid again, with a happy family. I want my sister back.

Very truly, I tell you, you will weep and mourn, but the world will rejoice; you will have pain, but your pain will turn into joy.

JOHN 16:20

INTO THE PIT

~ LONELY

I lie awake;
  I am like a lonely bird on the housetop.

Psalm 102:7

I made the arrangements. I notified the rest of the family. After the funeral, I finished packing up and cleaning. I wrote and mailed the thank-you notes.

Now that I've gone back to work, I don't know what to do next. I don't know how to deal with the emptiness and numbness that I feel. I am like an automaton going through the motions. I don't know what to do.

I have passed out of mind like one who is dead;

I have become like a broken vessel.

PSALM 31:12

CAR WASH

I washed the car today.
It was so lonely. There was nobody to squirt me
with the hose or squeal with delight when he
plunged his hands into the bucket of soapy water.
Nobody said with pride, "Look at what a good job I
am doing on this side, Daddy."

I think I'll just take the car to the car wash next time.
I miss him so much.

Save me, O God,

   for the waters have come up to my neck.

I sink in deep mire,

   where there is no foothold;

I have come into deep waters,

   and the flood sweeps over me.

PSALM 69:1–2

The Two-Step

When she was little, she would stand on my feet and "dance" with me. After we rocked back and forth in an exaggerated two-step for a while, she would lift up her head and grin at me, saying, "Twirl me, Daddy, twirl me." Then we would spin around the living room until we both collapsed into a fit of dizzy giggles. She loved to dance with me and never seemed to think I was awkward on the dance floor. With her I felt like Fred Astaire. I miss my little dancer.

The joy of our hearts has ceased;

our dancing has been turned to mourning.

LAMENTATIONS 5:15

LONELY

~ 192

*C*hurch is particularly hard. We have always gone to the Mass with the children's liturgy. Now it is painful to attend that Mass and sit near the families we have worshiped next to for so many years. Our church family should be one of our greatest supports in tragedy, but as it turns out, we do not even have that. It is too painful.

O send out your light and your truth;

　　let them lead me;

let them bring me to your holy hill

　　and to your dwelling.

Then I will go to the altar of God,

　　to God my exceeding joy;

and I will praise you with the harp,

　　O God, my God.

*H*e hadn't lived at home for many years, not since shortly after college. He was married, with children of his own. I was really proud of him. He was a good husband and father, a real success. He wasn't supposed to die before I did or before his children were grown. I feel lost and lonely without him, and very old.

I will seek the lost, and I will bring back the strayed,
and I will bind up the injured, and I will strengthen
the weak.

EZEKIEL 34:16

LONELY

$\sim$ 196

My precious little girl—how can she be gone? She was so beautiful, inside and out. Her goodness was part of what made her so beautiful. I used to be afraid that she would fall in love with somebody who wouldn't be able to see beyond her stunning physical beauty and appreciate her for the good and loving person she was. She was a precious jewel among the many gifts that God has given me. Without her shining radiance, life is dim and lackluster.

You are precious in my sight,
  and honored, and I love you.

ISAIAH 43:4

197 ~

LONELY

I seem to always be eating something. I'm not really hungry, and nothing tastes good, but I just keep eating without really thinking about it. I guess I'm trying to fill the emptiness that's inside me. It doesn't help, of course. I never feel satisfied, so I eat something else. Eating is something to help fill the time and keep me busy.

My soul thirsts for God,

for the living God.

When shall I come and behold

the face of God?

PSALM 42:2

At first a good many of our friends reached out to us in some way. They sent cards, brought food, and let us know they were praying—especially right after he got sick. As time went on, a few faithful friends stuck with us, but we have had contact with very few since the funeral. Our grief makes people uncomfortable. No one wants to think about a child dying. It's too horrible for people to realize that it could have happened to them. It's too close to home. Our lives used to be just like theirs. The easiest thing for them to do is avoid us and try not to think about it. I understand, but grief is lonely enough in itself.

Do not avoid those who weep,

but mourn with those who mourn.

SIRACH 7:34

LONELY

*O*nce when I was little, I got separated from my mom in a store. It was just for a few minutes, but it was really scary. Everything looked a little familiar, but I wasn't sure which way to go to get back to her. I feel kind of like that now, as if I'm lost in my own life, even in my own home. Everything looks familiar, but I don't seem to know the way to get back to safety or the way life is supposed to be. That day in the store, Mom was looking for me, too; and in a very short time she found me and hugged me tight, and everything was OK again. I am feeling lost now. I hope somebody finds me soon and makes everything OK.

For the Son of Man came to seek out and to save the lost.

LUKE 19:10

*S*leep is elusive. It comes slowly and stays only a short while. I lie awake feeling sad and lonely. This great void in my life is actually palpable. I feel it pressing on my chest and throat during the dark, wakeful hours of the night. I feel so alone. Do you hear me, God?

O LORD, God of my salvation,

when, at night, I cry out in your presence,

let my prayer come before you;

incline your ear to my cry.

For my soul is full of troubles,

and my life draws near to Sheol.

PSALM 88:1–3

I wish I had gotten down on the floor and played with him more. I regret the times when I didn't take the time to color a picture with him or march with him in the parade he led with his pot-lid cymbals. So often I didn't pause to build blocks or play trucks with him. I thought it was important to keep the house clean and the laundry caught up. I was busy trying to give him a nice stable environment, a peaceful home. Without him the house is clean and quiet, cold and empty. A little chaos would be great about now.

The mirth of the timbrels is stilled,

    the noise of the jubilant has ceased,

    the mirth of the lyre is stilled.

Isaiah 24:8

LONELY

*T*he flowers are coming out: crocuses and daffodils, tulips and dogwoods, even dandelions and crabgrass. He always used to bring me flowers, and I'd put them in a small cut-glass vase.

When he was little, he brought in fistfuls of wilted dandelions and crabgrass, or tulips and daffodils with stubby little stems.

Once when he was older, after he got his first part-time job, he brought me a bouquet of mixed flowers from the grocery store just to say, "I love you!" His flowers always came with a grin and lots of love.

I would give anything for a bunch of wilted dandelions now—if only I could see that grin again.

He has sent me to bring good news to the oppressed,

    to bind up the brokenhearted, . . .

to provide for those who mourn in Zion—

    to give them a garland instead of ashes,

the oil of gladness instead of mourning,

    the mantle of praise instead of a faint spirit.

ISAIAH 61:1, 3

I feel so alone without her. She was always with me. She accompanied me on all my errands: post office, grocery store, bank, dry cleaner, hardware store, pharmacy. She "helped" me with all my chores: sweeping floors, making beds, dusting furniture, cooking. Between chores we would read books together or have a tea party or play with her dolls or swing. Then we would snuggle close, and I would rock her and kiss her and put her down to sleep. She was part of everything I did, my constant little companion. How can I do anything without her? I wish she were here.

~ 210

Turn to me and be gracious to me,
  for I am lonely and afflicted.
Relieve the troubles of my heart,
  and bring me out of my distress.

PSALM 25:16–17

~ 212

With her around, life was like a banquet of exotic flavors that changed from day to day. When she was sixteen there was a drama almost every day. Either something wonderful happened or something terrible happened. A slight from a friend, a good grade on a test or project, or a piece of mail could make a day horrible or wonderful. I miss her passion and her exuberance. I miss the excitement, both positive and negative, that bounded through the door with her. She brought flavor and spice into our days. It's so dull here now; the world has become flat and tasteless. Only the bitter taste of pain remains.

O taste and see that the LORD is good;

   happy are those who take refuge in him.

PSALM 34:8

LONELY

*O*ur grief seems to come in waves. Unfortunately, our peaks and troughs don't come at the same time. When I need to sit in the dark and pore over the pictures, my husband can't stand the memories they bring. When he's ready to go out and do something, I don't want to leave the house. I thought we would at least have each other to share our grief with. How can grief be so different for two parents of the same child? I was counting on him to walk beside me on this journey of grief. I thought we could best help each other through this horror, but instead we seem to be on completely different wavelengths most of the time. We need each other but don't know how to help each other. We are on two different paths, and both are steep and rocky. It is my hope that someday our paths will again

converge, and we can walk side by side, holding on
to each other.

For the waves of death encompassed me,
the torrents of perdition assailed me.

2 Samuel 22:5

We lived in different states and didn't see each other very often, but I knew that she would be there whenever I needed her. She was the one I could talk to when I was young and confused and couldn't talk to our parents. She was the one I always wanted to share good news with first. She was the one I talked to when times were hard. I could always trust her to listen and gently guide me, loving me all the while. I didn't call her very often. I'm not sure if she knew how special she was to me or how much I needed her to be there. I never actually told her that she was my favorite sister, because it didn't seem right to have favorites. I feel as though my special, secret lifeline has been cut.

~ 216

For she knows and understands all things,

and she will guide me wisely in my actions

and guard me with her glory.

WISDOM 9:11

It is springtime, a time of new life. But for me, it is only a time of new death. The daffodils and azaleas don't move me. I feel cold and lonely. The spring sunshine fails to warm me. Jokes aren't funny, and music isn't beautiful. I feel flat and wooden, and I don't care. My child's death has changed every fiber of my life. I will never be the same.

A mortal, born of woman,

few of days and full of trouble,

comes up like a flower and withers,

flees like a shadow and does not last.

JOB 14:1–2

Mom and Dad's anniversary is coming up, and I want to do something really great for them. If I could just think of something that would make them feel happy for a few hours. I wish I could carry their burden of grief for a while so that they could really have a good time and maybe even laugh like they used to. I miss the way we all used to laugh.

Let your father and mother be glad;

let her who bore you rejoice.

PROVERBS 23:25

I wish I could be you, so that everybody wouldn't miss you so much, but I just don't have your talents. I can't tell jokes and make people laugh the way you did. I can't make friends and help everybody feel comfortable the way you could. I can't make Mom laugh the way you sometimes would when she was trying to scold us, and I am nothing like you in school. Everybody misses you, especially me, but I just can't be you. I wish I could. I wish somebody could. Then maybe we wouldn't miss you so much. Really though, nobody I know could ever be any good at being you.

But by the grace of God I am what I am, and his grace toward me has not been in vain.

1 CORINTHIANS 15:10

LONELY

*I*t is cold and windy as I look out on the barren world, and my heart feels colder than the frozen day, gripped by the icy hand of grief. There are icicles hanging down from the awning over the porch. They remind me of when he was only four or five and was so fascinated by those glittering columns of ice. We had to break them off and keep them in the freezer for him that winter. He was far beyond fascination with icicles when he died so many years later, but that winter nothing was more wonderful to him than icicles.

It has been a long time since I thought about that winter, but the memory makes me smile a little. As I look outside I realize that the sun has come out and the icicles are beginning to drip. Maybe there is some hope.

My soul melts away for sorrow;

   strengthen me according to your word.

~ ENDURING

*Indeed we call blessed those who showed
endurance. You have heard of the endurance of
Job, and you have seen the purpose of the Lord,
how the Lord is compassionate and merciful.*

JAMES 5·11

*S*omehow we endured the funeral, thinking that it would be the hardest part, simply because we couldn't let ourselves think beyond it. Now we must endure the pain that goes with missing her every day. Over and over, one day after another, she still is not here, and she won't be coming home. Will it ever get better? When will we find peace?

You need endurance to do the will of God and receive what he has promised.

HEBREWS 10:36 (NAB)

*D*ay after day goes by, one after another. We measure our lives in relation to his death. We date things in our minds as "before he died" or "after he died." The calendar pages slowly come off. It's been a week since he died, then a month. The months pass slowly without him. Why don't I feel better yet?

~ 230

Teach us to count our days

   that we may gain a wise heart.

PSALM 90:12

~ 232

I couldn't find my brief-case. I had been preparing all week for a big presentation, and there was just a little more paperwork to do—but I couldn't find my briefcase. I searched the house. I drove back to the office and looked everywhere. Then I finally found it behind the driver's seat of the car. This isn't like me. I don't usually lose things. I can't seem to remember anything since she died. I am often confused and unsure of even simple everyday things. I am afraid that I am losing my mind.

For I, the LORD your God,

hold your right hand;

it is I who say to you, "Do not fear,

I will help you."

ISAIAH 41:13

*E*very day is Halloween, in a way. Every day I put on my mask that says "I am OK," completing my disguise. I disguise myself as a normal person who is coping well. It is all a lie. Very few people know of my disguise, and even they see it come off only occasionally. It's tiring to lead a double life. I don't think I was meant for a life on the stage, but it's gone on so long now that most people wouldn't recognize me without my disguise. Perhaps someday I'll grow comfortable in my costume. It's beginning to fray around the edges from so much wear.

Why do you pretend to be another? For I am charged with heavy tidings for you.

1 KINGS 14:6

*I*t happened again today. I was about a mile from the house, and I realized that I didn't know where I was going. The grocery store? The dry cleaner? The mall? A half mile later, I finally remembered that I was on my way to the hardware store.

I often find myself just standing somewhere, not knowing what I am supposed to be doing. Why did I come into the living room? What am I looking for in the refrigerator? If I walk into the grocery store without a list, I spend half my time wandering around trying to remember what I came in for. It's as if my mind won't hold on to a thought. It might be funny if it weren't so scary. I wonder if I am going crazy.

Trust in the LORD with all your heart,
and do not rely on your own insight.
In all your ways acknowledge him,
and he will make straight your paths.

ENDURING

I move from one day to
the next, managing, just barely, to force myself out
of bed and into the shower. I eat because it is what
I'm supposed to do. I go to work because I must. I
try not to think too much. I try not to feel too
much, and soon, thank goodness, another day is
over, and I can climb back into bed, spent from the
tension of forcing myself to live. I can't look ahead
yet, nor can I allow myself to remember. I simply
try to get through each minute of every day, each
day of every week, each week of every month,
putting one foot in front of the other. It is my hope
that with sheer repetition it will somehow get easier.

Blessed be the Lord,

who daily bears us up;

God is our salvation.

Our God is a God of salvation,

and to GOD, the Lord, belongs escape from death.   239 ~

PSALM 68:19—20

ENDURING

*T*he shower is my refuge. It is the only place where I can cry. I used to cry openly, but now everybody seems to think that I should be past that, that I shouldn't be crying anymore. They think it has been long enough, but how long is long enough? Who is to say? I only know that I still must cry sometimes. So I cry in the shower and late at night when everyone else is asleep. Everybody is tired of my grieving. Don't they know that I am tired of it, too?

Protect me, O God, for in you I take refuge.

PSALM 16:1

ENDURING

I don't want to live without my child. I don't want to be here anymore. Why can't I die, too? I am so very tired. I don't want to go on living. Whatever life I have left is too long.

~ 242

Hear, my child, and accept my words,

that the years of your life may be many.

PROVERBS 4:10

I don't know how to move through this. The path of life that seemed so clear before she died is now invisible to me. I don't know where to go or how. I feel so lost and alone sometimes, but I am trying to trust you, Lord, to show me how to live each day. Right now it is the only way I can get from one day to the next.

I will instruct you and teach you the way you should go;

I will counsel you with my eye upon you.

PSALM 32:8

245 ~

I got a call from the teacher today. My daughter is having trouble at school. She isn't keeping her mind on her school-work and sometimes doesn't pay attention to what is happening in the classroom. At other times she is disruptive to the other children, and she is showing inappropriate and highly emotional responses when she is corrected, sometimes lashing out in anger or bursting into tears.

I am experiencing the same difficulties at work. I can't concentrate on my job, and my coworkers find my grief disruptive. I wanted to tell my daughter's teacher this. I tried very hard not to show my anger or burst into tears while talking with her.

My darling little girl—how difficult for her to be burdened by a teacher who does not understand grief. I said that I would talk to my daughter, and I will. But I won't be saying what the teacher expects me to say. What a brave little girl she is. I wish she had told me about the trouble she is having at school.

Look, my eye has seen all this,
   my ear has heard and understood it.

JOB 13:1

TANGLED BALL OF PAIN

Can you hear me, God? Will you help me? I don't know what to do. I don't know how to feel better and move on with my life. Everybody says I have to move on, but I don't really know what they are talking about. I don't know how. Do they mean I am supposed to forget about my sister or pretend that she didn't die? That's ridiculous. Nobody could do that. I wish I could put down this grief and sadness and pain, but I don't know how. It is too tangled up with my sister and how much I love her. I can't put her down just because it hurts to carry the grief. She is still my sister, and I love her and need her in my life.

I know that she will always be with me in a special way. It's kind of like my love for her is wrapped up in a tangled ball of string that is my pain and sadness

LONGING FOR MY CHILD

and the part of me that misses her so much. Maybe as time goes on the ball of pain will unravel and get smaller; maybe then more of my sister and our love for each other will shine through. Maybe then it won't hurt so much. In the meantime, I'll just carry this ball she's wrapped up in and hope for it to get a little smaller and lighter as time goes by.

So you have pain now; but I will see you again, and your hearts will rejoice, and no one will take your joy from you.

JOHN 16:22

Most of the time I pretend that I am OK. Mom and Dad want me to be OK. It's really hard for them. They are so sad, and they miss her so much. I don't want them to have to worry about me, too. I wish it could be OK not to be OK.

~ 250

He will not wrangle or cry aloud,

nor will anyone hear his voice in the streets.

MATTHEW 12:19

ENDURING

I have come to dread all those places where you have to meet new people: PTA meetings, church socials, neighborhood block parties, long lines, the playground. The question always comes up: "How many children do you have?" It used to be such a simple question, but now I don't know how to answer it. I don't want to leave her out, but at the same time I can't stand to go over it again and again with every stranger I meet. I will never ask that question again as long as I live. Now I know how much it can hurt to have to answer it.

Be quick to hear,

   but deliberate in answering.

SIRACH 5:11

ENDURING

*T*ime has little meaning when it comes to grief and healing. When my child died, my very soul was ripped apart. Although months have passed, the pain is still very real. I trust that God is healing me, but it is a slow and painful process, slower and more painful than I could ever have imagined. People and books say that grief must not be rushed and that with the process comes healing, but I am tired of the pain and work of grief. I want it to be over. I want to know healing. I want to feel happiness again. It does not feel like this grief is healing me. It feels like it is destroying me. Help me to trust in your healing, God, and to really know that things happen for the good.

~ 254

Then they cried to the LORD in their trouble,

    and he saved them from their distress;

he sent out his word and healed them,

    and delivered them from destruction.

PSALM 107:19—20

~ FOREVER CHANGED

*In a moment, in the twinkling of an eye, . . . we
will be changed.*

1 CORINTHIANS 15:52

*T*he house is so quiet and still. There is no pounding of your feet as you run up and down the stairs at breakneck speed. Your CD player isn't blaring. There is no basketball thudding against the concrete or reverberating on the rim of the basket. The back door hardly ever opens anymore. More than anything, I miss the sound of your voice, especially your laugh. How can I stand the quiet?

Even in laughter the heart is sad,

and the end of joy is grief.

PROVERBS 14:13

*O*ur cozy home has always felt like a safe haven until now. But now nowhere feels safe and secure. It is as if evil has invaded like a dark and sinister mist. Nothing is sacred. Anything can happen. I feel vulnerable and afraid—and exposed.

Death has come up into our windows.

JEREMIAH 9:21

I don't know why I am so angry at my sister for dying. I know it's not her fault. She didn't choose to die. I'm so tired of having her dead. It hurts too much, and everything is changed. I feel like my whole life is ruined. I feel guilty for being so angry at her, and I know it doesn't make sense, but I can't help it. I'm mad at God, too. I wish everything could be like it was before, when we were just a normal happy family.

~ 262

And the LORD said, "Is it right for you to be angry?"

JONAH 4:4

*A*s the trees begin to
bud and now that spring is in the air, I realize how
very different my life was this time last year. I was
young and happy, with a wife I loved, a job I liked,
and a healthy and happy family. My life was full of
possibility, and I could see beauty all around me.
Now I am an old man who has seen evil and knows
heartache. I have learned the hard lessons of death
and misery, and I am forever changed.

I have been young, and now am old.

PSALM 37:25

265 ~

~ 266

*E*verything seems out of kilter, as if the world is tipped on a funny angle so that everything is off balance and nothing seems quite right. Rooms that should be full are empty. Places that should be noisy are quiet. Work that was stimulating and interesting is boring and meaningless. Nothing is right. Even the sunlight seems dimmer. I want everything back the way it was. I don't like this. I want to walk briskly and with confidence, secure in my life and my family. Instead I am scared.

I cry aloud to God,

aloud to God, that he may hear me.

In the day of my trouble I seek the Lord.

Psalm 77:1–2

267 ~

THE EMPTY CHAIR

*T*he chair sits empty at the supper table. It is a tangible symbol of all that is missing in our lives. It is a daily reminder that he is gone. Its emptiness fills the room and seeps into our hearts like a cold relentless fog—or maybe our hearts are the source of the emptiness that fills the room. I can't believe that my son is dead. I keep thinking that there should have been a way for us to prevent his death, but there was really nothing we could have done. I don't know if my wife blames me or if she thinks I blame her. Both of us say that there is no one to blame, but there is a cold emptiness between us, and I'm not sure where it is coming from or how to get rid of it. I am heartbroken, and I fear that in addition to losing our son we are losing each other. We don't know how to comfort each other. How can an empty chair make us feel so alone?

You will be missed, because your place will be empty.

1 Samuel 20:18

*H*ow much time I have
been wasting! I never realized it. I thought I was
being responsible and acting like a grown-up. I've
been working hard, putting in extra time at the
office, making a name for myself in the company.

~ 270

The death of my daughter has shocked me into
another kind of maturity. I know now how fragile
life is and how essential it is that I do the important
things—like hold my wife and spend time playing
with the children.

Lay aside immaturity, and live,

and walk in the way of insight.

PROVERBS 9:6

I want justice for the person who did this. Well, maybe I want vengeance—I don't want mercy or lenience or the endless parade of lawyers and psychologists or the multiple delays of the justice system. I want justice, swift and sure.

Will not God grant justice to his chosen ones who cry to him day and night? Will he delay long in helping them? I tell you, he will quickly grant justice to them.

LUKE 18:7–8

*M*y child's death has given me a new perspective on life. I no longer spend extra hours at the office. I try to focus on good things and to use well the time I have. I hold my wife's hand and take the time to really listen to her. We need each other more than ever now. I wish I had done all this while my little one was still here. I miss that kid so much.

Enjoy life with the wife whom you love.

ECCLESIASTES 9:9

*I*t's the little things that I miss the most. I never could get the hang of french braiding. Mine always came out bumpy or crooked. She used to always braid my hair for me. It felt so good when she brushed it and braided it. It always made me feel pretty. She knew how to do everything, and she tried to teach me. I know it sounds selfish to think of the things that she used to do for me, but that's who she was. She was a person who helped me and did things for me. I miss her so much.

~ 276

Through such works you have taught your people
that the righteous must be kind,
and you have filled your children with good hope.

WISDOM 12:19

277 ~

My friends think I'm avoiding them. I guess I am. It's just that the things that are important to them seem so trivial to me now. Clothes, football games, who broke up with whom, music, schoolwork—it all seems meaningless to me now and completely unimportant. I just don't want to spend the energy pretending that I care about that stuff anymore. I'm just not interested. I feel like I'm suddenly older than all my friends.

It is not the old that are wise,

  nor the aged that understand what is right.

JOB 32:9

I keep waiting to hear
the bang of the screen door, the thump of school-
books landing on the dining-room table, and the
creak of the refrigerator door. I don't even realize
that I am waiting for familiar sounds that I won't
hear again.

~ 280

I wait for the LORD, my soul waits,

and in his word I hope;

my soul waits for the Lord

more than those who watch for the morning.

PSALM 130:5—6

~ 282

*W*e prayed so long for a child, and for many years it was to no avail. We feared that we would always be childless. When we learned that a baby was coming, we rejoiced like we never had before. She was never a disappointment but only a joy. After waiting so long, everything about her seemed like a blessing—even dirty diapers, temper tantrums, raging adolescent hormones, braces, and tuition bills. I guess we should be thankful for the short time we had with her—and we are. But having had her here, we are so very aware of what we are missing now that we are childless again.

For this child I prayed; and the L ORD *has granted me*

the petition that I made to him.

1 S AMUEL 1:27

I feel as though I have been robbed, not only of my children but of my whole life as I knew it. So many of the things we did revolved around our lives as parents. Not only is everything different at home in all our day-to-day activities, but it's different everywhere else, in everything we do. We did things with other families and went to Scouts and PTA. If we went out to eat, it was to a family or fast-food restaurant, someplace that the children would enjoy.

With the children gone, we seem to have very little in common with most of our friends, even though we are the same people we have always been. They seem to be very uncomfortable around us, and I can feel us drifting apart. It is difficult to be in the family-type places that we used to frequent and to see all those happy families. We no longer have a reason to go to many of those places, such as the playground or the soccer field.

Our children are gone and so, it seems, are our entire lives: the ways we spent our days, the places we went, and the people we did things with.

I will come like a thief, and you will not know at what hour I will come to you.

285 ~

Revelation 3:3

I never knew how much I relied on your being here. I need an older brother. I'm not supposed to be the oldest. Having you around made me feel safe somehow. I don't know exactly why I don't feel safe without you, but I don't. I feel so lost. My leader is gone.

~ 286

He said, "Do not fear, greatly beloved, you are safe.
Be strong and courageous!" When he spoke to me, I
was strengthened.

DANIEL 10:19

I always wanted my own
room, but now that I have it I hate it. I miss my
brother. Yes, he was irritating sometimes, and
sometimes we didn't get along, but most of the
time he was great. We played together and talked
about things. I wish I could talk to him now. He
would have some answers for me.

*Hear my voice, L*ORD*, when I call;*

  have mercy on me and answer me.

PSALM 27:7 (NAB)

I used to believe that a lifetime was a long time. The years of my childhood, in retrospect, seem so long and happy, with plenty of time to explore and play and grow up. Then I had the relaxed and happy years of young adulthood: making lifelong friends, establishing a career, meeting the love of my life, and starting a life together. Now I'm so aware of each year sliding by quickly. I am aware of my own mortality and of how easy it is to lose my beloved family. I want to hold and cherish each moment that we have together, because I know, now, that they are so few.

You have made my days a few handbreadths,
    and my lifetime is as nothing in your sight.
Surely everyone stands as a mere breath.

PSALM 39:5

291 ~

FOREVER CHANGED

~ GLIMMERS
OF HOPE

Let your steadfast love, O LORD, be upon us,
even as we hope in you.

PSALM 33:22

BLAME

I want to blame somebody. I want to lash out in my bitterness and point to someone and say, "It is your fault." I want reparation and reprisals and vengeance for the life of this innocent child, but there is no good in this kind of railing. I can't even blame God. The God that I have known and loved all my life would never harm a child. I don't know what to do with my anger and my malice, but somehow I know in my heart that they have no real place in my grief for my son. It sullies his innocence to dwell on these emotions.

*Put away from you all bitterness and wrath and anger
and wrangling and slander, together with all malice,
and be kind to one another, tenderhearted, forgiving
one another, as God in Christ has forgiven you.*

EPHESIANS 4:31–32

*S*ometimes I think I just can't bear it. I have very little will to go on, don't know how to proceed, and have no strength to continue. Then some small thing will happen that allows me to inch forward just a little: someone is kind, someone needs me, or for a brief moment I become aware of something beautiful around me. I am graced with a glimpse of light and a flash of hope in this tunnel of grief, and I am able to take one more step toward what I hope is the other end of it.

No trial has come to you but what is human. God is faithful and will not let you be tried beyond your strength; but with the trial he will also provide a way out, so that you may be able to bear it.

1 CORINTHIANS 10:13 (NAB)

*I*t was a beautiful fall day. The air was crisp and fresh and the sun was shining brightly. The leaves were brilliant shades of gold and red and orange. I looked out the window of my gloomy house and was dazzled by the glorious view. I had to stand there for a few minutes, just drinking in the vibrant beauty of the hills and the sky. I felt refreshed and invigorated, in spite of my broken heart.

Great are the works of the LORD,

to be treasured for all their delights.

PSALM 111:2 (NAB)

299 ~

I noticed the flowers today. I guess they have been blooming for a while, but today I finally noticed them. Maybe I am beginning to live again. I still feel both pain and numbness, but I noticed the flowers today. Thank you, God, for their beauty.

For now the winter is past,

the rain is over and gone.

The flowers appear on the earth;

the time of singing has come,

and the voice of the turtledove

is heard in our land.

SONG OF SOLOMON 2:11–12

We hold each other with tenderness. Our lovemaking means more now than it ever has. It represents everything our life together has become. It contains our joy and our sorrow, our delight and our passion. We support each other during this time of sadness. Even though our lovemaking is bittersweet, it nourishes us and helps us to go on. How I need you now, my precious love.

~ 302

Sheepfolds and orchards bring flourishing health;

but better than either, a devoted wife;

Wine and music delight the soul,

but better than either, conjugal love.

SIRACH 40:19–20 (NAB)

*S*ometimes I am sure that she is still here and that she can see and hear me. Every once in a while I can feel her close to me. I can't explain it, but it is a peaceful, comforting feeling, as if she is here just to be close to me and help me feel better. It doesn't happen very often, mostly when I am missing her very badly and feeling really terrible. Maybe I am imagining it, but I don't think so. Maybe it is my guardian angel comforting me or God giving me a little caress, but it feels like my sister, standing beside me again, for just a moment.

He said, "My presence will go with you, and I will give you rest."

$\mathbf{M}$om and Dad are
really sad, and I don't know how to make them
happy again. I'm sad, too, and I miss my little
sister, but I want to tell them that it's going to be
all right. Sometimes I'm afraid to let them know
when I'm happy about something, because I sort
of think that maybe I'm not supposed to be happy.
After all, my sister died—but she was always happy.
I don't think she would want them to be so sad. I
wish they could be happy with me.

~ 306

Happy are those who love you,

and happy are those who rejoice in your prosperity.

Happy also are all people who grieve with you

because of your afflictions;

for they will rejoice with you

and witness all your glory forever.

Tobit 13:14

I slipped into church for a quiet prayer. It was empty, but I was not alone. I felt your presence, Lord, and the sun seemed to be shining more brightly when I came out.

~ 308

How lovely is your dwelling place,

O LORD of hosts!

PSALM 84:1

We went to a support group for parents whose children have died. At first I was apprehensive about going. I've never been a support group type of person, and I thought we would be uncomfortable. But they were kind, and they listened and understood.

Looking back on the meeting, I don't know why I feel better, but I do. I'm going to go again next month.

God is faithful; by him you were called into the fel-lowship of his Son, Jesus Christ our Lord.

1 CORINTHIANS 1:9

*W*e stopped at the overlook and stretched our legs. The view of the valley was stupendous, with smoky blue mountains all around. It was peaceful, and the leaves were a riot of color and light. She would have loved this place. The parking area was ringed with huge boulders. We all scrambled to the top and took in the magnificence of the scene. The towns and buildings looked tiny from there. Even our own troubles seemed small in the majesty of the mountains. When we got back in the car we all felt refreshed.

Great are the works of the LORD,

    studied by all who delight in them.

PSALM 111:2

*T*here are many memories, and they are constantly with me. Every room and almost every object triggers another memory. At odd moments a sound or a look will remind me of something about him or of something he did. At first these reminders made me cry (I was crying all the time), but now I treasure them. They are not enough; they don't make missing him any less painful. But I'm glad to have my memories.

Mary treasured all these words and pondered them in her heart.

LUKE 2:19

315 ~

I know that you are with me, Lord. I have felt your presence throughout this horrible ordeal. I know that you have been sustaining me. Don't desert me now. Somehow I think the worst is yet to come in the long days and nights that will follow. Please help me through my grief. Help me that I may live day by day without my child. I need you, Lord.

~ 316

Let your steadfast love become my comfort

according to your promise to your servant.

Let your mercy come to me, that I may live.

PSALM 119:76—77

I picked up my Bible today and thumbed through it. I was surprised by how many passages spoke to my heart and seemed to apply to me right now. I found comfort, strength, and nourishment.

~ 318

I commend you to God and to that gracious word of his that can build you up and give you the inheritance among all who are consecrated.

ACTS 20:32 (NAB)

*O*ur friends have rallied around us to provide support. They offer to help in any way. In the sadness of their eyes and in their faithful service through this long ordeal, I can see how they care. There's really not much that they can do, but they assure us of their constant prayers. It helps to know that these good people are praying for us. Thank you for the blessing of friends, Lord.

~ 320

May your friends be like the sun as it rises in its might.

JUDGES 5:31

*S*ometimes I think that if she could see us now, she would be disappointed in us. I don't think she would want us to be this sad. She would say, "Be happy." She was happy and exuberant, full of life and hope and excitement. There was nothing quiet or somber about her. She would be fed up with all this sadness and gloom. She would want to go and have a picnic and run and jump and dance and laugh. Maybe I'll ask Mom if we can go on a picnic soon.

A time to weep, and a time to laugh;
a time to mourn, and a time to dance.

ECCLESIASTES 3:4

*S*he collected pennies. She kept them in a huge plastic duck bank. The bank was almost full when she died. "They are up to his neck!" she said excitedly as she put the last ones in. We all gave her our pennies, along with any we found under the sofa cushions or on the street. Now as pennies accumulate in my wallet, I don't know what to do with them. I spend them as quickly as I can because they remind me of her. But every now and then, when I'm feeling really low, I find a penny unexpectedly, often right next to the car or in some other odd place. It makes me feel as if I'm getting a special hello from my little girl, and it encourages me.

Let the little children come to me, and do not stop them; for it is to such as these that the kingdom of heaven belongs.

Matthew 19:14

THE BLUE SHIRT

Whe I got around to the laundry, I discovered that his favorite blue shirt was in the bottom of the hamper. I left it there. I just couldn't wash it that day. Every time I got down to the bottom of the hamper again, I saw it and left it. At first, seeing it made me sad, but as time went on I began to see it as a little part of him that remained, and after a while, seeing it in the bottom of the hamper made me smile and feel closer to him.

O LORD my God, I cried to you for help,

and you have healed me.

PSALM 30:2

327 ~

I still cannot see anything good in the death of my child, but I have begun to be able to see the good in what remains of my life. Thank you for the gifts you have given me, Lord. Thank you for my ability to love. Thank you for my strength. I didn't know I could bear something like this. Thank you for my husband. He is my support. Thank you for my other children and for my faith. They give me hope.

But by the grace of God I am what I am, and his grace toward me has not been in vain.

1 CORINTHIANS 15:10

*T*he cafeteria was crowded, and there weren't many empty tables. Not long after we sat down I caught a strong whiff of tangerines. I suddenly remembered how much she enjoyed them—smiling delightedly as she peeled back the skin, separated each section, and popped it into her mouth. I realized that I was smiling as I remembered, and I was not trying to hold back tears. I knew I had turned some kind of corner in my grief. I was beginning to find comfort.

~ 330

Blessed are they who mourn,

for they will be comforted.

MATTHEW 5:4 (NAB)

~ FINDING BLESSINGS

You bestow on him blessings forever;
you make him glad with the joy of your presence.

PSALM 21:6

We never dreamed
when we got married that this would be one of the
things we would have to endure together. I've heard
that adversity tears some couples apart and makes
others stronger. I don't know what this will do to us;
I only know that I need my husband's love forever. I
couldn't get through this without him.

[Love] bears all things, believes all things, hopes all things, endures all things.

Love never ends.

1 CORINTHIANS 13:7–8

335 ~

I look at my wife and marvel at her strength. She has been through so much and has emerged stronger and more beautiful than ever. Her face shows the lines of the hardships she has borne, but her smile and her quiet strength bring her a beauty and dignity like none other. It's good to hear her laughter begin to return. I am so grateful for and humbled by her love for me.

Strength and dignity are her clothing,

and she laughs at the time to come.

PROVERBS 31:25

I am so grateful for the time we had with him. Every moment and every memory is precious. If God hadn't sent him into our lives, we would never have known the pure joy of his love, and we would never have known what we are missing. Even though the loss of him is excruciatingly painful, it is worth the pain of missing him just to have had him, known him, and loved him.

Only you know, God, how he enriched our lives and how impoverished we are now without him. We look forward to joining him again, in heaven.

I will give thanks to the LORD with my whole heart.

PSALM 9:1

~ 340

W hen the children
were little and one of us was tired or at the end of
our rope, the other would always pick up the slack,
laugh, and say, "Now I know why God gives children
two parents." How much truer it is now. We sustain
and encourage each other every day. I couldn't
survive this without my spouse, my helpmate,
my love.

Two are better than one, because they have a good reward for their toil. For if they fall, one will lift up the other; but woe to one who is alone and falls and does not have another to help.

ECCLESIASTES 4:9—10

*H*e was good-looking and very photogenic. His picture on my desk created quite a stir. People were always telling me how handsome he was. What they didn't know was that he was also very kind, gentle, and so smart that it was almost scary. He was a bundle of so many talents and so much love that I know he could have done great things if only he had been able to live long enough. He did great things within the family; but in a few more years he would have taken on the world.

He had a son whose name was Saul, a handsome

young man. There was not a man among the people of

Israel more handsome than he; he stood head and

shoulders above everyone else.

1 SAMUEL 9:2

I once met a lady whose teenaged son had been killed several years before in an automobile accident when another driver went through a red light. She was so full of faith and seemed so at peace with his death. She said that he had had a troubled youth and had been heavily involved with drugs and other bad things, but that finally, about a year before he died, he had completely turned his life around. He had gotten clean and sober, had found a deep and abiding faith in God, and had spent his time giving talks in high schools and youth groups, trying to convince other kids to avoid the mistakes he had made. She was obviously very proud of him. She quietly told me that although it was very difficult for her to lose him, she believed that God, who knew what was to come in her son's life, had allowed him to die when he was most happy and closest to God. She said that if her son had lived, perhaps he would have become discouraged and lost his faith or returned to his old ways. She said that she had realized that his eternal happiness was more important to her than having him with her for a few more years here on earth.

I have thought of her often since my child died, and I marvel at her faith. I am trying to develop faith like that, but I haven't gotten there yet.

I know, O LORD, that your judgments are right,
    and that in faithfulness you have humbled me.
Let your steadfast love become my comfort
    according to your promise to your servant.

PSALM 119:75—76

She wasn't listed in a Who's Who. She never won an award or even a contest. She never had her name in the paper. She was too young to have many biographical facts. She had no occupation, hobbies, club memberships, volunteer work, or extracurricular activities. She didn't even have an alma mater. Her life was so short that the only mark she made in the world was on our hearts. Not many people knew her, but those of us who did will never forget her.

All those things have vanished . . .

like a ship that sails through the billowy water,

and when it has passed no trace can be found,

no track of its keel in the waves.

Wisdom 5:9–10

I wouldn't trade a minute of it. I cherish every moment I had with my little girl. No matter how painful the memories are now, they are all precious. I wish there were more of them. Her little life was so radiant, so full of sparkle and light. She brought us such great joy. When she was very sick, she continued to be brave and cheerful. Her concern was for us, even then. What an extraordinary child she was. We are blessed to have had her, even for a short time.

For this child I prayed; and the LORD has granted me the petition that I made to him.

1 SAMUEL 1:27

*O*ur friends have been wonderful. They brought food to the hospital, and other times they sat with us and listened, or cried with us, or held our hands. They have been available at a moment's notice to watch after our other children and have provided distractions, fun, and food for them. They have prayed with us and for us. How can we ever thank them?

~ 350

Faithful friends are beyond price;

no amount can balance their worth.

Faithful friends are life-saving medicine.

SIRACH 6:15—16

351 ~

My friends have been great. They understand my moods and have been patient with and kind to me. They let me talk when I need to, and they understand when I don't really feel like talking or doing things. They have even cried with me. Best of all, they have talked about my brother, sharing the things they remember about him and the things we all did together. I'm lucky to have good friends.

Faithful friends are a sturdy shelter:

whoever finds one has found a treasure.

SIRACH 6:14

We got together with our cousins last week. At first it was a little awkward. We hadn't seen them since the funeral. Soon, though, we started to relax and have a good time together. The best part was when everybody started telling funny stories about my brother. We laughed and laughed about the fun things he had done and the funny things he had said. We were missing him, but—for a change—it was a fun kind of missing him.

And whoever does not provide for relatives, and espe-cially for family members, has denied the faith and is worse than an unbeliever.

1 TIMOTHY 5:8

*N*ow that some time has gone by, I can see that my family (at least what's left of it) is closer. We stick together more. We like to be with one another. We are even stronger. We are closer to one another—and closer to God, too. We are more focused on what is important. We do things differently now. We are more spontaneous and less formal. My parents are not as strict about things like being proper and neat and making sure that everything looks right to other people. I think we are kinder and gentler than we used to be. We even fight a little less. Life is less hectic and more peaceful. Sometimes we are still very sad, but now we can be happy sometimes, too.

And after you have suffered for a little while, the God of all grace, who has called you to his eternal glory in Christ, will himself restore, support, strengthen, and establish you.

1 PETER 5:10

~ GOOD DAYS,
BAD DAYS

This is the day that the LORD has made;
let us rejoice and be glad in it.

PSALM 118:24

~ 360

W

e had a wonderful day today. The whole family went to a very special place: an old Victorian estate with a mansion and beautiful grounds that is now maintained as a park for the city. It is a peaceful refuge. We had a picnic and took time to really relax. We lay in the grass and looked at the clouds. After a while we played an invigorating game of hide-and-seek among the big shady trees. We ran and jumped and chased each other, and laughed and laughed. I can't remember the last time we had so much fun.

He makes me lie down in green pastures;

he leads me beside still waters;

he restores my soul.

PSALM 23:2—3

SMALL PIECES

I keep finding small toy parts—little Lego pieces, odd blocks, game pieces, puzzle pieces—the way you find pine needles stuck in the rug and in corners for months after Christmas. I keep thinking that I have put away or gotten rid of everything; and then, unexpectedly, something else pops up, just as my grief does. I keep thinking that I am doing better, that I am more in control and am coming to terms with his death. And then something or nothing triggers my grief, it over-whelms me again, and I know that I am not in control at all. I'm broken into so many small pieces. Can I ever heal?

Restore us to yourself, O LORD, that we may be restored;

renew our days as of old.

LAMENTATIONS 5:21

The Kite

When he was little he was so proud of "flying" his kite. He was afraid to let out the string, so he would run as fast as he could, holding tightly to the string four feet from the kite. Up it would go, four feet over his head. He would look over his shoulder as he ran, grinning because his kite was "flying." When he slowed down or turned, it would come fluttering or crashing down, and he would take off running again. I just couldn't get him to understand that if he let out more string he could stop running and his kite would soar. He was afraid that it would fly away.

Am I like that—clinging to my grief and my memories, refusing to let go and live and soar, afraid to lose the little of him that I have? That is the pattern of my grief: flying briefly on a good day, then crashing down again and again. But just as he was not yet ready to let out his string so that his kite could really fly, I can't let go now. I have more to experience and more to learn before I can move on. I am afraid, too. It doesn't help when others tell me it is time to move on, any more than it helped for me to tell him to let out the string.

On other March days, in later years, he was ready and able to let go and really fly his kites, and they would soar heavenward until they were only dots in the sky. I will be ready one day, too—but it won't be this March.

The wind blows where it chooses, and you hear the sound of it, but you do not know where it comes from or where it goes. So it is with everyone who is born of the Spirit.

JOHN 3:8

~ 366

I remember that when he was little he used to grin and pose whenever he saw a camera. It was impossible to get a candid picture of him. I remember that from the time he was about eight or nine he had a corny joke to share for every occasion. I remember how he looked before his morning shower, with his hair sticking up as he shuffled into the kitchen to give me a hug and have breakfast. I sure miss those morning hugs and those corny jokes and grins.

His mother treasured all these things in her heart.

LUKE 2:51

*S*ome mornings I wake up feeling good, just like I used to. The sun is shining, the air is cool, the sheets are crisp. I stretch, and then I remember. How could I have forgotten? She is dead. It is a new day, but its troubles are the same as yesterday's. Help me to thank you for this new day, God. Help me to offer you all my prayers, works, joys, and sufferings today. I feel tired and beaten down already. Please help me today, God.

Hear my words, O LORD;

listen to my sighing.

Hear my cry for help,

my king, my God!

To you I pray, O LORD;

at dawn you will hear my cry;

at dawn I will plead before you and wait.

PSALM 5:2–4 (NAB)

*T*his year I participated in the "Walk for a Cure." I didn't know anything about this disease until my son was diagnosed. Even though it's too late to help him, I want to do what I can to increase awareness and raise money for research so that other mothers' sons won't have to die of this painful disease. I felt connected with the people at the walk. We were all working together for a worthy cause. There were other parents there whose children had died, and some whose kids were still living with the disease. My heart went out to them, because I knew what they still had ahead of them. It felt good to be part of something so important. Everybody there was so kind and hopeful; we had a great time together, and I felt a kinship that went beyond family. I came home feeling tired but very good. Maybe I

~ 370

can do more as a volunteer for this cause. I want
to do something important. I want to help make
something good come from this tragedy.

For you have delivered my soul from death,
  and my feet from falling,
so that I may walk before God
  in the light of life.

PSALM 56:13

DIVERSION

*I*t has been a hard month. It's always difficult around the anniversary of his death. We went out with another family last Saturday, though, and we really enjoyed ourselves. These friends had no idea they were inviting us out on the anniversary of our son's death—and of course we didn't mention it. The day's activity was just the diversion we needed. We didn't forget, but we really did have fun.

The steadfast love of the LORD never ceases,

his mercies never come to an end;

they are new every morning;

great is your faithfulness.

LAMENTATIONS 3:22—23

THE WEDDING

*T*he whole family gathered for my niece's wedding. It was the first time we had gotten together since the funeral. As I looked at my parents, who are in their eighties, and saw all that their union had wrought, I was aware more than ever of the hole that now exists in the family tree. With our son's death a whole branch has been pruned away. Even though the family now numbers more than thirty-five and still counting, everybody seemed to miss him at the wedding. I think of others—my own grandchildren and great-grandchildren—who will never be.

So the wedding was turned into mourning and the voice of their musicians into a funeral dirge.

1 MACCABEES 9:41

*T*oday would have been her birthday. I remember so many others: the parties, the cakes, the decorations, the presents, the excitement and anticipation—all the traditions that were so special to her. I also remember the other birthdays, the ones that are scattered through the long stretch of loneliness since she died. She has now been dead longer than she was alive. I still miss her so much. How can I celebrate today?

Why is one day more important than another,

when it is the sun that lights up every day?

SIRACH 33:7 (NAB)

*T*he holidays are really hard. We talked as a family about what we wanted to do. Do we want to do the same things and continue our traditions? Will it hurt too much? Should we try something completely different? Should we have some things the same and some things different? How should I know what we are going to be capable of? It seems that everything is ruined, even all the holidays. Isn't it enough to have your sister die? Why do Thanksgiving, Christmas, birthdays, Easter, and every single thing have to be ruined? Will anything ever be really good again?

Your festivals shall be turned into mourning,

and all your songs into lamentation.

T O B I T   2 : 6

*T*oday was a pretty good day. I was out shooting a few hoops, and some friends came by. A good game developed, and I concentrated on playing my best. I really gave it everything I've got. I completely forgot about you for a little while and actually felt good when I was

~ 380

playing and afterward. I was tired, but it was a different kind of tired: hot and sweaty and muscle weary, normal and healthy, like before you died. It felt good to get the blood moving again instead of just being so tired from grieving and missing you. I felt a little guilty that I forgot about you for a while and actually had fun, but then I realized that you wouldn't want me to feel guilty; you would be glad. I took a shower and knew that today was a good day.

He drew me up from the desolate pit,
out of the miry bog,
and set my feet upon a rock,
making my steps secure.

PSALM 40:2

*L*ast week we went to a party that my boss hosted. I was amazed by the number of people who were complaining about their children. One man was going on about the weird girl his son was dating and his fear that his son would never grow up and move away. Another woman was sure that her children were going to drive her crazy before the holiday break was over. She couldn't wait to get them back to school and out of her hair. There were many groans and nods of agreement from most of the guests as they complained about their children and commiserated with others. We didn't say anything at the party but talked about it on the way home. Why did they seem so eager to be rid of their children? Don't they know that each moment they have with their children is a treasure that can't be replaced?

For where your treasure is, there your heart will be also.

LUKE 12:34

I was appalled to realize today that I am still angry at you for dying so many years ago. Mother is becoming very frail. Soon we will have to make arrangements for her to leave the house that has been her home for so long. You were always so much better with her. You would be able to help her see the reality of the situation. From you, she could take it. You are supposed to be here to handle this. I know it was an accident. I know it wasn't your fault. I know you didn't choose to die, but I still need you and miss you so much, even after all these years.

But with whom was he angry forty years?

HEBREWS 3:17

~ FINALLY
SURVIVING

Very truly, I tell you, you will weep and mourn,
but the world will rejoice; you will have pain, but
your pain will turn into joy.

JOHN 16:20

*O*ur lives have changed completely, but somehow we go on. We are surviving. There is still a lot that we don't understand. Some of it we just had to let go of, and some of it we still puzzle over from time to time. Life goes on, we do what we need to do, and eventually it gets a little easier. God has not abandoned us, and we have found our way back to him. There are pockets of hope and more and more moments of happiness. We have not been destroyed, only changed.

We are afflicted in every way, but not crushed; per-plexed, but not driven to despair; persecuted, but not forsaken; struck down, but not destroyed.

2 CORINTHIANS 4:8—9

*T*here is a Scripture verse—Romans 8:28—that people like to quote in the face of tragedy. I know that they are trying to be helpful, but most of the time this kind of platitude just makes me want to slap them. Instead, I clench my teeth and try to smile, at least a little, because of their good intentions. They seem to be saying that there can be something good in the death of a child.

This is not about finding a "silver lining" in something horrible or about having a "good attitude." I have come to the realization that after a time we can be called to make something good come out of such a tragedy. The good comes when we can use our experiences and our pain to help others or in some way improve ourselves and the world according

to God's purpose. It is what we do with what we
have been dealt that matters.

*We know that all things work together for good for
those who love God, who are called according to
his purpose.*

ROMANS 8:28

I don't know when things started to change, but gradually I found myself smiling, then laughing, then wanting to be with people instead of dreading them. The terrible pain has diminished to a dull ache. I still have days full of tears, but they are less frequent now. I can honestly say that I have many days of happiness and joy.

You have turned my mourning into dancing;

you have taken off my sackcloth

and clothed me with joy.

Psalm 30:11

FINALLY SURVIVING

*I*t has been a while now since my sister died. The things that used to hurt so much—seeing and doing her favorite things, going to her favorite places, looking at her picture—feel much more comfortable now. I still have an aching longing for her, but I find myself smiling more when I think of her, instead of crying. I'm glad she's no longer sick or in pain. I still miss her very much, but even more than that, I am happy that she was my sister. I am happy for the time we had together, even though it was so short.

Sing for joy, O heavens, and exult, O earth;
  break forth, O mountains, into singing!
For the LORD has comforted his people,
  and will have compassion on his suffering ones.

ISAIAH 49:13

I try to concentrate on what I have instead of dwelling on what I have lost. I miss my child as much as ever, but I know I have been given many gifts and blessings. I am blessed to have known her. She was a beautiful woman, inside and out, and it is a great blessing to have had her in my life. I have a devoted spouse, loving children, and genuine friends. I was raised by parents who loved me. I live in peace and freedom, in a warm house with plenty to eat and meaningful work to do. I have my faith and the knowledge that God loves me. I have much to be thankful for and am constantly reminded of these blessings when I look around at the brokenness in the world. I see people whose families and countries are torn apart by hatred, war, and famine. I am grateful. I did nothing to deserve being born into my circumstances. I want to be content with the blessings that I have been given.

Be content with what you have; for he has said, "I will never leave you or forsake you."

HEBREWS 13:5

397 ~

We have started a new tradition in her memory. We make lots of cookies during the seasons that meant the most to her. She especially loved Easter and the time of year when the leaves on the trees are full of vibrant color. At these times we take plates full of cookies to several neighbors who either are too busy to bake or are elderly and have no one to bake for anymore. When we can, we take a big box to our neighborhood nursing home. We don't tell anyone that they are in her memory; we just spend a few minutes visiting, being sure to smile and be cheerful. She had a way of sharing a smile with everyone around her and giving them a lift. We try to do the same as we deliver our cookies. We feel good when we have delivered them. It's amazing how giving to others who are lonely can take away our own emptiness.

Your prayers and your alms have ascended as a
memorial before God.

ACTS 10:4

399 ~

*T*omorrow I will graduate. I wish you could be here to see it. These last few years without you have been very tough. At first it was so terrible that I didn't know how I would ever get through it. Gradually the days got a little better, and I finally decided that I would live in a way that would make you proud of me. That helped me to go on and to try to be a better me. Now I am proud of myself. I think you would like me and be proud of me, too. I would trade anything to have you back, but I can truly say that I have survived and grown and become stronger. I think I have a better idea of what is really important, and that has helped me to make better choices and to become a better person. Thank you for being someone whom I wanted to make proud of me. Thank you for helping me to become a better me.

~ 400

For I sent you out with sorrow and weeping,
*   but God will give you back to me with joy and*
*   gladness forever.*

BARUCH 4:23

We planted a rose garden as a memorial to our children. Red roses for Bobby, pink for Jenny, yellow for Tina, and white for John.

I've never been much of a gardener, but I enjoy tending to the roses. I look forward to being able to sit in the garden surrounded by the fragrance of the roses and to be at peace. I like to cut the roses and put them in a vase in the kitchen so that I can see them and smell them as I prepare dinner. The fragrance of the roses pervades the room, and I feel a little closer to my missing children.

How glorious he was. . . .

Like roses in the days of first fruits,

   like lilies by a spring of water,

   like a green shoot on Lebanon on a summer day.

403 ~

SIRACH 50:5, 8

FINALLY SURVIVING

After a while, what helps the most is to do something for other people. We started out buying some books for our local support group for bereaved parents. At other times we submitted an article or poem to the newsletter. It's hard, but somebody has to be there to help and listen to newly bereaved parents. The only way to really move through the pain and sorrow and ultimately have any kind of life is to try to find something good in the tragedy or make something good come from it. Every parent finds his or her own way, in his or her own time, but reaching out to others finally helps more than anything.

The merciful lend to their neighbors;

by holding out a helping hand they keep the

commandments.

SIRACH 29:1

405 ~

*E*ven though he was my little brother, now he is my guide. When I am in a tough situation or don't feel like doing what is right, I often think about what he would do or what he would want me to do or say. He was a good person. I want to be good like he was, so I think about what he would want me to do, and it's a little easier to do the right thing. He was so brave and kind when he was sick, and he was sick for a long time. I was sure he would get better, and he did, for a while, but then he got worse again. I miss him. I am not nearly as brave as he was. I like to think of him being my little guide. I think I'm only making it because he is sharing his courage with me now.

For wisdom will come into your heart,

and knowledge will be pleasant to your soul;

prudence will watch over you;

and understanding will guard you.

PROVERBS 2:10–11

407 ~

I would like for the whole world to know about my wonderful son. I wish I could tell everyone of his kindness and goodness. I would like to build a memorial to him that would last for generations and make the world better, as he did.

I don't have the means to name a building for him or to endow a scholarship in his name. I can plant a tree or design a Web site, but I can also share his goodness with the world in everyday ways. When I have a particularly difficult task ahead of me, I offer my effort as a prayerful tribute and memorial to my son and as a prayer offering for his eternal happiness. I find that I do a better job on the tasks that I quietly do in his name. Sometimes this kind of prayer in action makes the task easier, too. I am also beginning to offer good times as a memorial to him and prayer for him; I do this when we are having a great day on a family outing or when I see something that I'd like to share with him.

This kind of memorial won't let the world know his name or how good he was, but it is something that I can do every day to make the world better in his memory.

I do not cease to give thanks for you as I remember you in my prayers.

EPHESIANS 1:16

RESOURCES

The Compassionate Friends
PO Box 3696
Oak Brook, IL 60522-3696
(630) 990-0010
1-877-969-0010
http://www.compassionatefriends.org

TCF Canadian National Office
PO Box 141 RPO Corydon
Winnipeg, MB
Canada R3M 3S7
(204) 475-9527
1-866-823-0141
E-mail: tcfcanada@aol.com
http://www.compassionatefriends.org

Mothers against Drunk Driving (MADD)
PO Box 541688
Dallas, TX 75354-1688
1-800-GET-MADD
http://www.madd.org

MADD Canada
  6507C Mississauga Rd.
  Mississauga, ON
  Canada L5N 1A6
  1-800-665-MADD
  http://www.madd.ca

National Organization of Parents of Murdered Children, Inc.
  100 East Eighth St., Suite B-41
  Cincinnati, OH 45202
  (513) 721-5683
  1-888-818-POMC
  http://www.pomc.com

411 ~

American Association of Suicidology
  4201 Connecticut Ave., NW, Suite 408
  Washington, D.C. 20008
  (202) 237 2280
  http://www.suicidology.org

The National Hospice and Palliative Care Organization
  1700 Diagonal Rd., Suite 300
  Alexandria, VA 22314
  1-800-658-8898 (Help Line)
  http://www.nhpco.org

Bereaved Parents of the USA (BP/USA)
National Office
PO Box 95
Park Forest, IL 60466
Fax: (708) 748-9184
http://www.bereavedparentsusa.org

SIDS Alliance
1314 Bedford Ave., Suite 210
Baltimore, MD 21208
(410) 653-8226
1-800-221-7437
http://www.sidsalliance.org

Pen-Parents
http://www.penparents.org

Alive Alone
11115 Dull Robinson Rd.
Van Wert, OH 45891
(419) 238-7879
http://www.alivealone.org

In Loving Memory
  1416 Green Run Ln.
  Reston, VA 20190
  (703) 435-0608
  E-mail: inlvmemory@aol.com
  http://www.inlovingmemoryonline.org

SHARE Pregnancy and Infant Loss Support, Inc.
  National Office
  St. Joseph Health Center
  300 First Capitol Dr.
  St. Charles, MO 63301-2893
  (636) 947-6164
  1-800-821-6819
  http://www.nationalshareoffice.com

Office for Victims of Crime, U.S. Department of Justice
  810 7th St., NW
  Washington, D.C. 20531
  1-800-331-0075
  1-800-833-6885
  http://www.ojp.usdoj.gov/ovc

Bereaved Families of Ontario
  36 Eglinton Ave. West, Suite 602
  Toronto, ON
  Canada M4R 1A1
  (416) 440-0290
  http://www.bereavedfamilies.net

Center for Loss and Life Transition
  3735 Broken Bow Rd.
  Fort Collins, CO 80526
  (970) 226-6050
  http://www.centerforloss.com

TAG: Teen Age Grief, Inc.
  PO Box 220034
  Newhall, CA 91322-0034
  (661) 253-1932
  http://www.smartlink.net/~tag

Dougy Center for Grieving Children
  3909 SE 52nd Ave.
  PO Box 86852
  Portland, OR 97286
  (503) 775-5683
  http://www.dougy.org

Chris Lafser has endured the death of four of her children. She makes her home in Virginia with her husband, Bill, and her three surviving children, whom she homeschools.

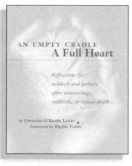